# CLINICAL PRACTICE
# AND
# THE ARCHITECTURE
# OF THE MIND

Robert Langs

# CLINICAL PRACTICE AND THE ARCHITECTURE OF THE MIND

*Robert Langs*

Foreword by
*Arthur H. Feiner*

London
KARNAC BOOKS

First published in English in 1995 by
H. Karnac (Books) Ltd.
58 Gloucester Road
London SW7 4QY

Copyright © 1995 by Robert Langs

The rights of Robert Langs to be identified as author of this work have been asserted in accordance with §§ 77 and 78 of the Copyright Design and Patents Act 1988.

All rights reserved. No part of this publication may be reproduced, stored in a retrieval system, or transmitted in any form or by any means, electronic, mechanical, photocopying, recording, or otherwise, without the prior permission of the publisher.

**British Library Cataloguing in Publication Data**

Langs, Robert
    Clinical Practice and the Architecture
    of the Mind
    I. Title
    616.8914

    ISBN 1 85575 088 0

Printed in Great Britain by BPC Wheatons Ltd, Exeter

# CONTENTS

FOREWORD by Arthur H. Feiner — vii

### Part I
### Observation and architecture

1  The fundamentals of psychotherapy — 3

2  Some basic tenets — 10

3  Issues of adaptation for patients and therapists — 17

### Part II
### Pursuing the design of the mind

4  The classical models of the mind — 31

5  The communicative-adaptational model of the mind — 41

| | | |
|---|---|---|
| **6** | Some features of the emotion-processing mind | 52 |
| **7** | The conscious system of the mind | 65 |
| **8** | Probing the deep unconscious system of the mind | 80 |
| **9** | Essential features of the deep unconscious system | 97 |

## Part III
## Consequences of the architecture of the mind

| | | |
|---|---|---|
| **10** | Techniques of therapy and the design of the mind | 113 |
| **11** | Syndromes of dysfunctional design | 124 |

| | |
|---|---|
| *REFERENCES* | 143 |
| *INDEX* | 145 |

# FOREWORD

*Arthur H. Feiner, Ph.D.*

I first became familiar with Robert Langs's work when, as editor of *Contemporary Psychoanalysis*, a paper of his about collusion and misalliances caught my eye. It was an exciting introduction to his work. We began publishing his writings in 1975, and continued to do so enthusiastically, because we believe Langs has something to say to all psychotherapists. This current volume is the culmination of all his seminal thinking: his is a fecund mind at work. And it is a labour of love, growing out of more than 30 years' interest in the theory and dynamics of psychotherapeutic practice and his desire to base psychoanalysis and psychotherapy on the realities of what goes on communicatively between patient and therapist, and what goes on intrapsychically in each as well.

Dr Langs was trained as an orthodox psychoanalyst. In addition to his clinical experience and acumen and training, he has the further enviable gift of being a prodigious writer of clarity and incisiveness. This aspect of his evident talents is reflected in the many papers and books he has published or has edited, as well as their outstanding merit and the originality of their contributions.

Early in his career, following the production of a two-volume exposition of psychoanalytic theory and technique, Langs began trenchant revisions and extensions, which eventuated in what he called an adaptational–interactional point of view, with its particular emphasis on frame maintenance.

With this current publication he has gone beyond that in an attempt to describe the structure of the human mind and how it reveals itself in empowered psychotherapy, which is his term for his evolved, now matured, communicational approach. Since he is clear that his conclusions come from what is evident in the therapeutic process, what he writes is immediately applicable as a powerful contribution to therapeutic action.

Any study of the human mind requires that we look at how humans interpret their worlds. This book echoes that dictum as an interpretation of the human acts of interpretation. The study is difficult because as researchers we are caught in a dilemma. Our minds are the object of study as well as the agent of the study. This means that our struggle to describe the limitations of the human mind is itself subject to those limitations and blind spots. Fortunately, Langs courageously moves in this direction, sometimes subjecting himself to the same scrutiny.

With any knowledge comes awe and mystery, if we take the time to look deeply enough. And with this brilliant effort—more wondering, producing more knowledge—we are seduced into penetrating deeper and deeper into the labyrinth of our being. As therapists, this is where we need to go. If the physicist can tell us that the atoms of our brains are constantly being replaced—that is, the ones that were there a week ago are not there now—we can legitimately ask: what is the mind? How is it possible that the atoms of today remember and react to what went on with the atoms of a year ago, atoms that have long ago been replaced? There is no easy answer.

Although therapists probably take it for granted, one of the more remarkable things that Langs has discovered is that our deep unconscious processing system is largely in contradistinction to our conscious system, which functions practically, keeping us oriented towards the real world. We often respond consciously to negative stimuli (e.g. therapists' mistaken interventions) with endorsement and, much to our chagrin, even by asking for more of the same. On the other hand, our deep unconscious system seems ever available to protest against these self-abusive, destructive situations. What this suggests is that self-definition has two parts. One functions homeostatically in the world around, defensively perhaps; but the other—deeper, and far out of awareness—functions in a more visionary way, implying, not least, how things might be better. But the messages are cryptic and need careful monitoring and decoding, for them to be useful at all. Langs's contribution is particularly practical in that decoding search so that therapy and its purpose, change, becomes viable.

Man's uniqueness follows his growth as an individual dependably related to the history of his species. This is not a history reflected in genes and chromosomes but, rather, as J. Bruner points out, reflected in the culture external to him, and wider in scope than is embodied in any one person's view or experience. Therefore the growth of mind is always a growth encouraged and assisted from the outside. Langs's work, therefore, becomes a searchlight helpful in scrutinizing the real effects of our assumed assists in response to someone asking for help. The destructiveness as well as the expansiveness and enhancement of therapy, and how these are accomplished, are our responsibilities as a mini-cultural experience transcending the bounds of an individual's self-hurtfulness or competence. It seems logical, then, that the relief and transformation of the limits to growth depend on how therapy engages the individual in using his intellectual and emotional potential.

By spelling out the various meanings of decoded triggers, or those stimuli to which patient and therapist respond adaptationally, Langs has set us on a journey of exciting discovery. His reminder of the significance of the total setting of psychotherapy—the background framework, the therapists' interventions, as well as the patients' responses, and the patterning of these from session to session—sharpens our inquiry.

While we do not have any complete sense of all of the possibilities of the growth of a person, Langs's effort to reveal and understand the structure and the process of the mind can only be of immense value, a stimulus for more research, especially with the modern developments in neuroscience.

But what Langs calls the communicative approach to psychotherapy and a sensitivity to the adaptational aspects of the processing mind still stand, as he says, "without the full support of the therapeutic community". How unfortunate for the field of psychotherapy. And it is its loss. With the introduction of this study, its further clarification of clinical practice, and the structure of the emotion-processing mind, the field of psychotherapy may have a renewed opportunity to make the rectification needed to its own advantage.

*PART I*

# OBSERVATION AND ARCHITECTURE

CHAPTER ONE

# The fundamentals of psychotherapy

There is, I believe, a measure of dissatisfaction and a wish for more effective forms of psychotherapy lurking in the mind of every mental health practitioner. There have been many definitions of the unsolved mysteries and the ills that have befallen the psychotherapeutic realm and many prescriptions for their cure. Yet the plethora of diagnoses and amelioratives speaks more as symptoms of the disease rather than their solutions.

Virtually every book written about the theory and practice of dynamic psychotherapy and psychoanalysis (in this book, I do not distinguish between the two) carries with it the implied message: "These are the unresolved problems besetting our field, and here are some proposed solutions." With so many volumes written each year, is it possible to develop an overarching viewpoint that would bring order and sensibility to this maze of confusion and uncertainty? The belief that this quest can be fulfilled is the backbone of this book.

There seems little to be gained by trying to resolve this predicament by turning to one or another of the many current versions of psychoanalytic theory and invoking the seeming clinical insights it would offer. No single theory has gained primacy over its competitors or proven itself as a generally acceptable guide to clinical practice. My own efforts to use the communicative approach to psychotherapy to clarify the treatment experience have met with considerable success, yet they stand without the full support of the therapeutic community (Langs, 1982, 1988, 1992a, 1993a). Another kind of strategy is called for, and it appears to lie in one direction alone—turning at long last to basics, the heretofore undefined *fundamentals of psychotherapy*.

To move in this direction, I propose that we deconstruct the process of psychotherapy into its cardinal elements and use these fundamentals as a new context for comprehending the transactions and dynamics of the clinical situation. An effort of this kind would be in keeping with recent work designed to develop a bottom-up science and theory of psychoanalysis that could supplement the top-down theory of Freud and his followers, with its stress on high-level, general concepts and broad generalizations (Langs, 1992c; Langs & Badalamenti, 1992).

Virtually all present-day psychoanalytic theories stress three elements:

1. *Individuality*—the uniqueness of each patient and therapist, and the therapeutic unfolding they create conjointly; the distinctiveness of each patient's genetic make-up and life history; and the special attributes of and basis for his or her psychopathology.
2. *Psychodynamics*—the role of interpersonal and intrapsychic conflict; issues of affect, self-image, and tension regulation and the like, as they pertain to both therapy and a patient's emotional dysfunctions.
3. *Broadly stated universals*—ill-defined attributes shared by all patients (and therapists) and their life histories, as well as all treatment interactions; generalizations that are formulated in dynamic terms, such as the Oedipus complex, transference, and resistance, which are broadly defined empirically and difficult to specify.

The shift to *basics* involves complementing these individually oriented perspectives with two additional considerations:

1. *Specific universals*—well-defined aspects of human nature that apply to all humans, patients and therapists alike, as well as to all therapeutic interactions.
2. In particular, for our purposes, *the fundamental structure and functions of the human mind*—the evolved general design and capacities of the human psyche that shape, constrain, and provide the resources for individual adaptations to emotionally charged impingements and for the processing of psychodynamically charged inputs.

In developing the interplay between the basic structure and universal attributes of the human mind on the one hand, and the individuality of patients and therapists on the other, we are adopting a new way of observing and thinking about the therapeutic process and its curative powers. It is within this integrated context that the clinical explorations of the present volume will unfold.

For some time now, evolutionary-oriented psychotherapists have been attempting to investigate the evolved nature of human emotional functioning (for details, see Tooby & Cosmides, 1990, 1992; Slavin & Kriegman, 1992). In so doing, they embarked on a quest for universal evolutionary trends and their effects on given individuals with particular genetic make-ups and life histories. However, their work suffers considerably because they have been attempting to formulate evolutionary scenarios for the aforementioned highly complex entities like transference and resistance, without defining the more basic elements of the mind on which natural selection inevitably acts (Gould & Lewontin, 1979). They have thereby placed themselves in a position similar to trying to understand human language without a science of linguistics, or the human *brain* without any knowledge of its neuronal structure. Research of this kind requires the identification of basic components; so, too, with investigations of the human *mind*.

The search for fundamental components—irreducible structures and functions—typifies the pursuit of virtually all current forms of science, from physics and chemistry to anthropology and archaeology. Physics without a quest for the essential building blocks of matter is unthinkable, much as anthropology without the pursuit of the earliest forms of life and of the hominid line—and the essential features with which they are distinguished—would be incomprehensible. In practical terms, engineers could hardly think of building efficient and safe power plants without an understanding of basic physics. And despite all protests, the same principles apply to psychotherapy—we need to grasp our own essentials if we are going to forge effective and safe forms of treatment.

The need for a fundamental science of psychoanalysis has been recognized for some time, though there is considerable debate as to its feasibility (see Kuhn, 1962; Edelson, 1984; Grunbaum, 1984; Langs & Badalamenti, 1992). Recently, however, almost unnoticed, there has been a series of empirical efforts to shape psychoanalytic research and theory in ways that would qualify the field as a true part of science and biology (Langs, 1992c; Langs & Badalamenti, 1992, 1994). These endeavours range from formal research studies that have brought statistical and, more recently, stochastic and mathematical methods to psychoanalytic data, to important developments in human psychology shaped by evolutionary-oriented psychotherapists and psychologists (Tooby & Cosmides, 1990, 1992; Slavin & Kriegman, 1992).

While still in their infancy, these efforts at formal science and at identifying the genetic basis of emotional functioning, psychopathology, and the factors that influence the process of psychotherapy serve to remind us that human beings are very much a part of nature and that they can—and must—be understood deeply as such. Movement towards science inevitably brings with it the realization that basic mental structures and functions must exist—and that the promise held by identifying their design and operations should be pursued.

What, then, are the fundamentals of the therapeutic experience and the process of cure—of psychotherapeutic clinical practice? At first glance, this appears to be a surprisingly difficult question to answer. After all, we are dealing with an extremely complex aspect of nature, a multidimensional situation within which two individuals, each a complex entity, interact and strive to "cure" an equally complex dysfunction in one of them. Unfortunately, we do not have the "luxury" of investigating a single, readily defined—however complicated—identifiable structure or set of functions like vision or language, or even the brain. Instead, we are trying to study two *minds* in interaction, at a time when the investigation of the interplay between two more easily delimited *brains* barely exists.

Where, then, should we locate these mental basics? Within the patient, the therapist, or the system they create together? Or less broadly, do they reside in the respective psyches of one or both of these participants in treatment, or in their respective behaviours and communications, or in what each experiences subjectively and *consciously*, or in the nature of their respective *unconscious* experiences—whatever they may be? Or should we instead turn to the therapeutic setting, or to the ground rules and framework of the treatment experience, as our fundamentals? There appears to be a wide variety of basic entities that pertain to the therapeutic experience, ranging from aspects of each person to their systemic interplay with the setting in which the treatment transpires.

Each of these interacting domains has clinical relevance and impact, and each deserves intensive study. The immediate issue becomes one of deciding where to begin this examination of basics—which entity seems most promising? Because psychotherapy is essentially a human endeavour, we are likely to be inclined to concentrate our efforts on the patient and/or therapist—doing so as they experience and respond to each other's communications and to the conditions under which they are conveyed.

This option leads us to our next problem: patients and therapists are very complex individuals. We must therefore select some basic aspect of their structure and functions as a specific starting point for our sojourn into fundamentals. The choice that I have made is reflected in this book. For many reasons, I have elected to study what I term *the emotion-processing mind*—the complex configuration of *mental* (as distinguished from *brain*) structures and processes through which humans adapt to emotionally charged stimuli or impingements. Given that the *adapting mind* is central to human existence—and to psychopathology and its cure—*the architecture or design* of this mental configuration seems to be a logical and promising entity for first study.

How then can we develop a blueprint for the design of the emotion-processing mind*—and a delineation of its ramifications for clinical practice? Clearly, our definition of this structure and its functions will depend heavily on what we choose to observe, how we organize those observations, and the formulations we derive from these efforts. Both observation and interpretation will be necessary.

The field of observation that I have chosen to concentrate on is the therapeutic interaction and, more specifically, the communicative exchanges between patients and therapists. I make use of two clinical paradigms or settings in developing these studies: (1) *communicative psychotherapy*, and (2) its more recent off-shoot, *empowered psychotherapy*, which involves a basic, well-defined adaptive task for both the patient and the therapist (Langs, 1992a, 1993a). Furthermore, given that the patient free-associates and thereby reveals far more about the adaptive dynamics and structures of the mind than the therapist, who speaks only intermittently, I will be especially focused on the patient's contributions to the therapeutic dialogue—and only secondarily, though without neglect, on those of the therapist.

It is on this basis that I here derive a contemporaneous blueprint or model of the architecture of the mind, which, in turn, is used freshly to explore and comprehend the therapeutic experience and the process of cure. The interplay between model-making, on the one hand, and clinical practice, on the other, is at the heart of this book.

Join me now in an exploration of the design of the mind. I think you will be quite surprised at where this journey takes you and how it affects your understanding of psychotherapy

---

*The human mind appears to be organized into two basic systems—the *cognitive mind*, which is responsible for all adaptations that are *relatively emotion- or conflict-free*, and *the emotion-processing mind*, which is responsible for adaptations that involve emotionally charged inputs or stimuli. For ease of writing, I use the term "mind" in this book to refer to the *emotion-processing mind*, unless otherwise indicated.

and its methods. I, myself, as I pursued this path, was rather astonished by the realizations I was making and the directions they pointed to with respect to clinical practice (Langs, 1986, 1987a, 1987b, 1992c). It is my hope that this book aptly conveys the excitement of discovery that characterized these pursuits and, at the same time, gives vitality to the new clinical techniques and perspectives they speak for.

*CHAPTER TWO*

# Some basic tenets

Ms Allen is a young woman in once-weekly psychotherapy with Dr Barton, a clinical psychologist. She entered therapy mainly because she was repeatedly attracted to very hurtful and destructive men and had not been able to forge a satisfying and lasting relationship with any of them.\*

In the tenth month of her treatment, the patient began a session with a dream in which her father's brother, Martin, forces her to get into his car and drives her to a secluded place where he forces himself on her sexually. She went on to recall that Martin was an erratic man. At times he was

---

\*As is my practice, the vignettes in this book are fictitious illustrations but are, nevertheless, firmly based on clinical observation. This approach is necessitated by the inviolate right of all patients and therapists to total privacy and confidentiality for their therapeutic endeavours.

kind and helpful, but he had a violent temper and could be assaultive both verbally and physically to anyone in range of his wrath. Ms Allen remembered an incident in which he appeared unexpectedly at her home when she was a teenager. No one else was there at the time, and he made obscene remarks and seductive overtures towards her. Although quite frightened, she was able to get him to leave by pushing him out the door before anything more untoward occurred.

The uncle was a car mechanic who worked endless hours, even Sundays and holidays, a habit his wife and children strongly objected to and openly resented. He seemed more concerned about earning money—he had a morbid and unrealistic fear of poverty—than he was about his family and their needs. He really should have spent more time with his family, Ms Allen lamented. His daughter has had major problems with drugs, and these must have stemmed from his being away from home so often. There was also a suspicion in the family that he had been seductive with her and that perhaps they had had incestuous sexual contacts.

Ms Allen continued: The dream must have been prompted by a family gathering the previous weekend at which the uncle appeared and behaved provocatively. She kept out of his way and was glad she did; avoiding him was the only way to prevent something awful from happening with him.

Enough of him, Ms Allen commented, and she went on to say that she had done a very strange thing at work [she was an editor at a publishing firm]. She had made an appointment with an important author she was working with, and had said she'd see him on the fifteenth—not mentioning the day. It turned out that the fifteenth was a Sunday and that the author had come to her office on that day, thinking it odd but romantic. When he found her firm's offices closed, he became quite enraged, and Ms Allen had to endure a lot of flack when he called that Monday to complain about what had happened.

Ms Allen had meant to see him on Monday rather than Sunday, and she wondered if she was being unconsciously seductive in inadvertently proposing the Sunday meeting. It was a rather destructive thing to do—hurtful for both the author and herself. She wondered if she was threatened by the man's attractiveness; maybe she was sending him a mixed signal of wanting to be involved with him socially, while at the same time putting him off. In any case, it was a major blunder and she regretted her mistake.

This is a rather unremarkable segment of a psychotherapy session. The patient reports a dream and associates to it. There are narratives and emotional issues—a lot to digest and make deep sense of. It is the job of the therapist to formulate the *most compelling* meanings of these communications—those that are most pertinent to the vicissitudes of the patient's psychopathology (interpersonal or intrapsychic). Eventually, these formulations must be translated into curative interventions—be they appropriate silences, interpretations, and/or managing the ground rules or framework of the therapy at the behest of the patient's material. The nature of these efforts depends, as I pointed out in chapter one, on the therapist's approach to observing the therapeutic interaction and the ideas he or she derives from these observations. It is a vast landscape that tends to defy readily agreed-upon definition.

## *SOME BASIC TENETS*

To understand nature in any of its myriad of manifestations, we have no choice but to select for study those features we believe to be most cogent for comprehending its mysteries. We can then trace the vicissitudes of these observables, using them as a fair and telling representation of the behaviours and emotional issues we wish to explore. Inevitably, this selection process must be guided by a set of theoretical postulates and convictions that must be sound enough to allow for a productive choice of variables. On the other hand, the entire effort must leave room for openness and for the opportunity to make unforeseen observations that run counter to the guiding theory and call for fresh thinking.

As a rule, effective dimensions tend to involve ever-present variables that are relatively mundane yet profoundly capable of representing in deeply meaningful fashion the complex transactions that we intend to investigate. In this regard, the following can provide us with the minimal conceptual context we will need for studying the basic aspects of the therapeutic process that we will soon be concerned with:

1. *Human beings are adaptive organisms.*

The *strong adaptive viewpoint* states that both patients and therapists respond to specific emotionally charged stimuli—*impingements or triggers*—and they do so with a wide range of adaptive resources (Langs, 1992c, 1993a, 1993b, 1994, in press).

2. *Humans cope with emotionally charged triggers with both conscious and unconscious adaptations—behaviourally and communicatively.*

Human adaptation takes place on *two planes*—one with actual or potential awareness, and the other without such a possibility. We will take *unconscious adaptation* quite seriously, using that term to refer primarily to an elaborate unconscious system of the mind that is defined psychodynamically and in terms of the processing of emotionally charged information and meaning—and not apply the term to automatic adaptations and those that belong to direct and potentially conscious coping efforts.

3. *With regard to language or verbal communication, conscious adaptations are reflected in manifest, directly stated, surface messages, while unconscious adaptations are reflected in latent, indirectly stated, disguised or encoded messages.*

Human verbal communication (an observable of great importance to our efforts to fathom the design of the mind) is two-tiered—especially when it is conveyed in *narrative form.*

Storied communication is a means of conveying double messages, in that it consistently embodies two sets of meanings that reflect two distinctive levels of adaptation—conscious and unconscious.

At times, both the conscious and the unconscious adaptive responses have been activated by the same emotionally charged stimulus or trigger event. In these cases, the two-levelled response arises because the mind renders two rather different readings of the same trigger experience—one within awareness, and the other outside it. More often, however, the surface message deals with a *known (conscious) trigger experience*, while the latent or encoded message deals with a very *different trigger* which at the moment is *repressed and outside the awareness* of the message sender—and, typically, of the receiver as well.

In the clinical excerpt offered above, then, we would propose that the direct, manifest material reflects an adaptive response to seeing an uncle who at one time had behaved aggressively and seductively towards the patient. However, the indirect or encoded messages embodied in the same narrative recollections are likely to refer to *some other evocative emotionally charged experience*—one that Ms Allen is not aware of at the moment (nor are we as yet; see chapter five). *Unconscious adaptation typically involves an encoded adaptive response to a repressed, momentarily unrecognized, trigger event.*

4. *Adaptation is always direct and immediate.*

The evolved design of the adaptive capacities, physical and mental, of all living organisms centres on coping efforts that are responsive to immediate stimuli or triggers. This concentration on dealing first and foremost with contemporaneous stimuli applies to human mental adaptations, despite the highly developed capacities of humans to remember the past and to anticipate the future—and to deal with past traumas for long periods of time and anticipate and respond to future emotional issues far ahead of their occurrence.

While unresolved adaptive issues, past and future, may therefore evoke conscious—and, under selective conditions, unconscious—responses, coping with one's current environment, interactions, and impinging stimuli takes precedence adaptively. The most common configuration is one in which the present situation is the primary cause for adaptation, while related experiences, past and future, activate secondary coping responses largely because the present situation resembles or in some way calls forth experiences from other time-frames.

5. *Conscious adaptation is activated through conscious sensory experiences, while unconscious adaptation is activated by unconscious sensory experiences—subliminal or unconscious perceptions.*

In general, auditory and visual inputs are most critical on both levels of emotional adaptation. The key point is that our sensory apparatus operates along two tracts—one connected with awareness and the other completely divorced from it.

6. *As for therapy, then, the immediate interaction between patient and therapist is the primary source of adaptive responses for both parties, especially on the unconscious level of coping.*

For the patient, the therapist's interventions constitute the *primary* adaptation-evoking stimuli—and vice versa. All other adaptations reflected in the material from the patient and in the interventions of the therapist—responses to outside relationships and events, past, recent, and future—are *secondary* to the working over of the events and communications within the therapeutic interaction.

To avoid confusion, it is to be stressed that this does not imply that a patient's life outside therapy is inconsequential. The proposition merely states the empirically discovered finding that *the disguised or encoded communications from patients always reflect his or her unconscious coping responses to the therapist's interventions.* In general, the means by which a patient adapts to his or her therapist's interventions reflect his or her coping resources and their efficiencies and deficiencies—all of which have a bearing on adaptive efforts outside treatment and relate to the process of cure.

In summary, then, we will be striving to plumb the architecture of the human mind as it is designed for both conscious and unconscious adaptations to emotionally charged stimuli or triggers. As we do so, we will pay attention to the basic questions raised by these endeavours. For example, here at the outset, we may ask: what is the basic configuration of the emotion-processing mind? Is it designed so that these two realms of adaptation, conscious and unconscious, are handled by a single processing system—*the single-mind concept*? Or are there two distinctive coping systems, one attached to awareness and the other not—*the two-system, parallel-processing mind concept*? And if there are two coping systems, do they operate in integrated fashion or, oddly enough, quite separately? We are already raising novel questions about the human mind and its adaptations, and the answers are certain to bring us fresh understanding of the therapeutic experience.

CHAPTER THREE

# Issues of adaptation for patients and therapists

There are many settings within which we might profitably observe human nature in general and the human mind in particular. Among his many achievements, Freud invented a unique and remarkable setting within which the operations of the emotion-processing mind could be exquisitely investigated. Indeed, as far as I know, there is no better situation for the exploration of the adaptive capacities of the emotion-processing mind than that of dynamic forms of psychotherapy.

The psychological forces that are mobilized by a healer, and by the setting and rules within which he or she works with a patient, create a highly definable and compelling framework for the detailed scrutiny of adaptive interactions and the mental processes that underlie them. While each of the many variants on classical psychoanalysis has its own particular set of ground rules and boundary conditions—factors that affect what may be studied and how the studies are carried out—these situations also share a set of universal properties that, in addition to accounting for aspects of their curative powers, render them as ideal for clinical investigations.

In this book we mainly draw upon two analytically oriented settings for almost all our clinical observations. The first is *the communicative version of analytically oriented psychotherapy*—a setting I refer to as *the standard model of dynamically oriented psychotherapy* (Langs, 1992a). The second, termed *empowered psychotherapy* (Langs, 1993a), is a recent off-shoot of the communicative treatment paradigm. This latter variant was the product of a series of initial observations and formulations regarding the architecture of the mind that were made in the former situation. As it turned out, because this new form of therapy established an unprecedented field of psychotherapy observation with its own set of dynamics, work within the framework of its unique ground rules generated a number of fresh discoveries related to the very design of the mind that had given the paradigm its own beginnings.

## THE STANDARD COMMUNICATIVE SETTING

In order to understand the nature of our clinical observations and the inferences we draw from them regarding the design of the mind, we need to be clear about the conditions under which the observations were and will be made. As we would expect and will see, these formalities greatly affect the entire process that begins with clinical listening and observing and ends with a proposed model of the mind.

The standard communicative setting is optimally constituted by a private therapeutic space and a set of ideal ground rules. These rules may be summarized as follows (for details, see Langs, 1982, 1988, 1992a):

1. A private, sound-proofed office in a professional setting.
2. An exclusive two-person interaction.
3. A single, set fee; a set time for, and frequency of, sessions; a set length for each session; the patient's responsibility for the fee for all sessions for which the therapist is available; and the therapist's commitment to attend all scheduled sessions except for personal emergencies and a reasonable

number of vacation days. These tenets are termed *the fixed frame*.
4. The patient on the couch with the therapist on a chair set behind the couch where he or she is out of sight. (A viable alternative of face-to-face positions is possible as well.)
5. The patient asked to engage in unrestricted and unguided free associating—to say whatever comes to mind without censorship or direction from the therapist (compare this rule with its counterpart for empowered psychotherapy; see below). This tenet actually embraces two distinctive rules— that of *free association* (i.e. nondirected communication) and that of *saying whatever comes to mind without exception* (i.e. not editing the report of one's conscious thoughts and feelings).
6. Total privacy and total confidentiality.
7. The relative anonymity of the therapist, with no outside contact at any time between patient and therapist, no deliberate self-revelations by the therapist, and the therapist's commitment to intervene solely on the basis of the patient's material without introducing personal associations, biases, and the like.
8. The therapist's use of neutral interventions, namely those of appropriate silence, interactional or trigger-decoded interpretations, and managing the ground rules or framework of the therapy at the behest of the patient's encoded material (which will consistently direct the therapist towards frame-securing measures).

## *Adaptive issue within psychotherapy*

The therapeutic work and the responsibilities of both parties to therapy are defined by this treatment framework. The frame also defines the *specific adaptive tasks*—be they conscious or unconscious—that confront both the patient and therapist. These tasks must be clearly identified because, firstly, they are the issues that are being processed by the parties to therapy, and, secondly, in order to comprehend the adaptive resources and processing systems of the emotion-processing mind, we need a clear picture of what that mind is attempting to deal with.

The conditions of therapy, then, define a set of basic coping issues for each of the members of the treatment dyad. In addition, this framework also provides a context within which departures from the assigned tasks and from the ideal frame can be defined. These aberrations constitute a unique set of adaptive challenges that extend beyond those that would occur in the course of an ideally framed and conducted treatment situation. For the patient, they involve the therapist's frame modifications and his or her errant verbal–affective interventions and behaviours, while for the therapist they would involve any frame modification or rule-defying behaviour enacted by the patient (e.g. falling silent, concealing thoughts that come to mind during the session, introducing a third party into therapy, physically attacking the therapist, etc.).

## Adaptive issues for patients

As for the basic frame, the *conscious adaptive challenges* that it raises for the *patient* are to free-associate and reveal whatever comes to mind, attend to the therapist's interventions, and adhere to the ground rules of the therapy—e.g. to be in attendance for scheduled sessions, to pay the fee in timely fashion, to accept the time and length of the sessions, and such.

The recommendation that the patient adhere to these ground rules has a positive side to it in that doing so serves the interests of the patient by providing him or her with an optimal framework for the therapy, and with a measure of healing that is inherent to accepting a *secured or ideal frame*. At the same time, as we will see in some detail, this same healing frame evokes significant *secured-frame anxieties* (related mainly to fears of immobilization, helplessness, entrapment, and death). As a result, there is a traumatic aspect to this curative set of conditions, a conscious and more often unconscious anxiety that activates the patient's coping capacities and the adaptive systems of his or her emotion-processing mind.

We have in general tended to overlook the immediate adaptive tasks that confront both patients and therapists in every psychotherapy session—especially the latter. This oversight, which is both consciously and unconsciously motivated, stems from the *weak adaptive position* adopted by dynamic psychotherapists, one that affords only a vague sense of the adaptive issues that arise within the therapeutic setting. Another problem is the stress that these therapist's place on the intrapsychic issues of the patient—even when some activation by the therapist is recognized. This blind spot is further reinforced by a concentration on the past life of the patient and the genetic sources of his or her psychopathology—real factors in the patient's dysfunctions, but factors that are mistakenly invoked to *side-step the contemporaneous issues* between patients and therapists that exist at every moment of treatment. It is only when we adopt a *strong adaptive position* and begin to take seriously the centrality of coping with immediate, specific stimuli or triggers—whether consciously or unconsciously—that we are in a position to appreciate fully the coping issues confronting the two parties to therapy on an ongoing basis.

## Adaptive issues for therapists

For the *therapist*, the *conscious basic adaptive tasks* begin with his or her responsibility to create as ideal and secured a frame as possible for the beginning of a psychotherapy. This requisite proves to be a source of considerable *unconscious secured-frame anxiety* on his or her part and therefore a major, but generally unrecognized, adaptive issue (Langs, 1984–85). The therapist is also required to maintain the secured frame in as optimal a state as possible—assisted, as noted, by the encoded messages from the patient.

The therapist is also asked to be silent when the patient's material does not call for or allow an intervention, and to interpret the patient's encoded material, rendering its meanings conscious for the patient when that material permits—i.e. to interpret the unconscious adaptive meanings of the patient's free associations by identifying the key adaptation-evoking triggers and decoding the patient's responsive unconscious experience and coping efforts.

Sustaining appropriate silences is often consciously stressful for many therapists. Clearly, there is a set of underlying anxieties and issues that form the basis for this difficulty in coping soundly with uninterpretable material without an active response. Fears of passivity and helplessness, and especially a dread of the emergence of encoded, unconscious meaning, play a notable role in the maladaptive introduction of errant interventions during such interludes. Indeed, a therapist's silence in response to uninterpretable material is the single most effective means by which a patient's expression of material fraught with unconscious meaning is facilitated.

The task of interpreting to the patient is also by no means simply a cognitive issue for the therapist (Langs, 1984–85). At the centre of all validated interpretations are disturbing unconscious meanings, which are, in general, a reflection of incisive unconscious perceptions of the therapist in light of his or her interventions. Given the natural inclinations and training of today's dynamic psychotherapists, these perceptions are usually extremely distressing for all concerned. There is, in addition, a universal psychobiological defence against the conscious realization of deeply unconscious meanings that is unconsciously shared by both patients and therapists. For reasons involving both psychodynamics and the basic architecture of the mind, then, a therapist has a great deal to overcome and cope with, consciously and unconsciously, in the course of each and every psychotherapy session that he or she conducts.

In addition to these formal, frame-defined, and goal-directed tasks, both patient and therapist are *consciously* adapting to the behaviours and communications of the other. These *manifest responses* are often identified in terms of transference and countertransference, but it is well to recognize that they are *conscious and direct reactions* to the other member of the treatment dyad. In their surface manifestations, they lack an unconscious element that is, however, lurking in the disguised images each is experiencing and/or communicating (there is, of course, always an underlying unconscious component even when looking at surface phenomena).

Beyond these manifest concerns lies a host of latent adaptive issues that involve the ongoing *unconscious impingements* that patients and therapists *perceive subliminally*; these impingements evoke *unconscious* adaptive reactions that are eventually reflected in both *encoded* verbal communications and unconsciously motivated behaviours. In order to observe and formulate this level of experience, however, the *evocative triggers* for the encoded communications and behavioural coping responses must be identified. Indeed, activated disguised messages can be deciphered only in light of the stimuli to which they are a coping response.

Given the complexity of these emotionally charged triggers, it is helpful to have some general sense of the evocative—stressful/traumatic or healing—power of various interventions and frame-related impingements on the minds of both patients and therapists. These qualities are defined in terms of both individual sensitivities and universal responsiveness.

Here, too, as we struggle to define the nature and power of the stimuli that activate the emotion-processing mind, we must be open to discovering our errors and to unanticipated findings. Nevertheless, we must also have a reliable, non-blinding means of preparedness lest we find ourselves lost in a jungle of communicative material and adaptive issues. It is only with a sound grasp of the significant triggers to which the emotion-processing mind responds, both consciously and unconsciously, that we will be in a position to understand better the design of the mind that is reflected in these adaptive responses. This sensibility must, of course, be *empirically derived and unconsciously validated*, but in the course of our work here we will benefit from previous clinical determinations and insights.

As you might expect by now, ground-rule and frame-related triggers will loom large on our list of the strongest activators of the adaptive resources of the human mind. It will become apparent that the anxieties aroused by both secured and altered frames are among the most critical motivating forces in generating adaptive responses in both patients and therapists. Similarly, the dread of, and a natural inclination to obliterate, unconscious meanings also serves as an adaptation-evoking factor in the therapeutic situation (Langs, 1984–85). As the book unfolds, we will gradually develop a picture of the *primary adaptive tasks facing the emotion-processing mind in the psychotherapy situation*—and of the capacities that nature has fashioned to cope with them.

## EMPOWERED PSYCHOTHERAPY

Having offered a sense of the adaptive tasks inherent to dynamic forms of psychotherapy (communicative and otherwise), let us turn now to empowered psychotherapy in order to identify the additional coping issues created by its particular frame and structure. This mode of psychotherapy makes use of many of the ground rules of standard dynamic psychotherapy, but there are, as well, some major differences. The modality has a number of unusual features as a form of therapy, so the main effort here will be directed at offering a general sense of its design and the adaptive issues it creates (for details, see Langs, 1993a).

The following rules are distinctive to empowered psychotherapy:

1. The session is 90 minutes in duration rather than 45 or 50.
2. Because the therapy is structured within a quasi-educational framework, payment for the sessions is made in advance—usually for four-session units. The time is set aside for the patient, who can renew the sessions for as long as he or she wishes to do so.
3. The patient and therapist sit face to face, usually with a desk or another piece of furniture between them.
4. The patient is allotted the first 40 minutes of the session, during which the therapist is completely silent. During that time, the patient's assigned adaptive task is to complete a self-processing exercise—i.e. to begin with a dream or other narrative and end with a trigger-decoded insight (see below).
5. The patient is asked to follow *the rule of uncensored communication* (i.e. of saying everything that comes to mind), but

the rule of free and unencumbered associating (i.e. communicating without conscious purpose) does *not* prevail. This rule is replaced with *the rule of guided associating* (i.e. forcing associations to the elements of the original narrative) and with a specifically defined procedure for arriving at deep insight (see below for the rationale for this change).

6. The patient, as noted, is required to follow a relatively well-defined and specified series of steps designed to overcome the *natural resistances* against reaching into deep unconscious experience and adaptations. The steps in this process are:

   (a) Beginning the process with the report of a recent dream or with a short fictional story created spontaneously at the moment—the presentation of an *origination narrative* (the source of *guided associations*).

   (b) The development of a series of *guided associations* to the images in the origination narrative—the building up of a *narrative pool* of themes that includes both *bridging themes* (i.e. clues to adaptation-evoking triggers) and *power themes* (i.e. indications of strong unconscious issues—images that are openly sexual, damaging/death-related, or unrealistic).

   (c) The identification of the patient's emotional issues and especially *all of his or her recent impingements on the ground rules of the therapy*—i.e. actions that may be directed towards either securing or modifying the frame. This step is termed *listing patient-indicators*—i.e. indications of emotional disturbance or improvement in the patient.

   (d) The identification of the recent, active interventions by the therapist that are impinging on the patient, especially those that involve the ground rules of the treatment. This is termed *listing the recent triggers* that are activating the patient's adaptive responses.

   (e) Taking each strong trigger—i.e. intervention by the therapist—grasping its evident implications (especially in regard to whether the intervention secured or altered the frame), and then *linking* the themes in the patient's narrative pool to the implications of those interventions.

This reading of the connections between triggers and themes is structured as an interpretation that reveals the patient's *unconscious perceptions* of the therapist's effort. This step is called the *linking process or trigger-decoding*.

7. During the subsequent 50 minutes, the therapist intervenes actively in an effort to enable the patient, who almost never completes this process (it runs counter to the design of the mind), to fill in the missing pieces needed for effective linking and trigger-decoding—to arrive at true deep insight.

    (a) In general, the therapist's first efforts are directed towards identifying the specific ways in which the patient departed from the defined path of the process—e.g. a failure to generate sufficient guided associations or to list the active triggers or to carry out the linking process.

    (b) The second effort is directed towards having the patient fill in the gaps in the process so he or she can carry the exercise to completion.

    (c) Once a trigger-decoded interpretation has been made by either the patient or therapist, fresh guided associations are elicited from the patient. This new narrative is used to *assess the validity of the intervention*. In general, positive images and indirect or encoded extensions of the interpretation or frame-management (frame-securing) directive are confirmatory, while negative images tend to invalidate the intervention and call for reformulation.

The details of this process and its rationale have been presented elsewhere (Langs, 1993a). Of importance to our pursuit of uncovering the architecture of the mind is that this paradigm introduces a new and *specific adaptive task that consciously occupies the patient (and therapist) in each session*—to begin with a manifest narrative (usually a recent dream) and arrive at the conscious awareness of deeply unconscious perceptions, experiences, and adaptive solutions. Overall, then, the goal is to bring into awareness the unconscious phenomena that most powerfully affect our emotional lives.

In substance, the patient is asked to begin with a conscious image and end up entering his or her own deep unconscious mind in order to bring into awareness the deep understanding that exists on that level. The therapist shares in this task in that he or she must facilitate the patient's resolution of the inevitable resistances that are mobilized against achieving this goal by seeing to it that the most critical triggers have been identified and, with them, the patient's most powerful unconscious responses to those triggers.

Empowered psychotherapy provides the patient and the therapist—and us—with a unique opportunity to observe the emotion-processing mind in action, adapting to the task of discovering its own unconscious experience. The introduction of this particular goal gives this form of therapy a remarkable ability to reveal otherwise hidden aspects of the architecture of the mind. In addition, empowered psychotherapy has a great advantage over the standard models of therapy in that the techniques available to the therapist enhance the patient's expression of narrative material and thereby produce a maximum amount of encoded imagery. Similarly, the search for critical triggers is an active one and usually quite successful.

All in all, these features of the empowered process create a likelihood of achieving deep insight—of linking triggers and themes—that is far greater than that seen in standard therapies. Left to its own resources, the human mind tends to shy away from strong narrative imagery, from powerfully disturbing triggers, and from linking triggers to the themes so as to reveal its own deeply unconscious experience. Empowered psychotherapy was designed to overcome these naturally evolved universal tendencies. In many ways, then, this treatment paradigm offers a most opportune situation for investigating the architecture of the mind.

*PART II*

# PURSUING THE DESIGN OF THE MIND

*CHAPTER FOUR*

# The classical models of the mind

We have established two different settings for studying the architecture of the mind. We now need to define how we will attend to and formulate the communications from patients and therapists within these settings. Here, too, we must be selective. Trying to observe everything will only cause us to see nothing; on the other hand, however, what we do decide to study must be nondefensively chosen and fundamental, vital, and sufficiently critical to the therapeutic process and to its curative powers to reveal the structures, processes, and dynamics we seek to understand.

## MANIFEST OBSERVABLES

In light of our psychoanalytic approach, we wish to observe both surface phenomena and indications of nonsurface, unconscious transactions and communications. On the surface, there are the *manifest contents* of the patient's (and therapist's) spoken communications as they reflect the subjective state of the patient—and far more. Of special interest are the vicissitudes of the patient's emotional life and adaptive functioning—dysfunctions in these areas are the targets for therapeutic cure.

Attention to manifest, symptom-related *self-indicators* is supplemented by the consideration of ways in which the patient impinges on the ground rules or frame of his or her therapy—whether towards securing or towards modifying that frame. These manifest observables are signs of emotional health or disturbance in the patient, as well as reflections of pathological resistances or their absence.

The symptomatic and resistance maladaptations of the patient are the targets of the therapist's interventions. They are the *immediate disturbances in adaptation* that the therapist hopes to enable the patient to resolve insightfully. This is done through two means: (1) managing and securing the therapeutic frame as needed, and (2) offering validated interactional interpretations by linking activated triggers to encoded themes, thereby revealing the *unconscious experiences* that account for the patient's current dysfunctions or clinical improvement.

## FORMULATIONS OF MEANING

*Verbal-affective communication* has been selected as the main source of meaning and insight, conscious and unconscious, in our pursuit of the design of the mind. This choice was made largely because *human language* has been shown to be the distinctive carrier of *definable* encoded meaning, and the quantitative investigation of the communicative exchanges between patients and therapists was sufficiently powerful to yield a formal and lawful science of the mind (Langs, 1992c; Langs & Badalamenti, 1992, 1994). Other expressions of unconscious meaning—e.g. affect, subjective reports, body posture, etc.—are far more difficult to decipher and lack the specificity of an encoded message.

The processing systems of the human mind appear to be primarily language-based; even as these systems respond to nonverbal inputs, they unconsciously translate the incoming impressions into some kind of language-based meaning, which is then worked over consciously and/or unconsciously. It is extremely unlikely that the intricate and complex adaptations of the emotion-processing mind—and the structures through which these endeavours are carried out—could be adequately characterized on the basis of any source other than verbalized messages.

As noted, because patients engage in relatively uncensored and continuous communication, they will be our main (but not exclusive) source of clinical observations—data—for deriving the architecture of the mind. The *manifest contents* (and their evident implications) of patients' verbalized material will be used to formulate *conscious adaptations* in terms of *consciously experienced* triggers and direct, surface responses. This in turn will be used to characterize the system of the emotion-processing mind that deals with recognized triggers—issues that register in conscious awareness.

On the other hand, the latent or *encoded (disguised) contents* of a patient's verbalized material will be formulated mainly in terms of the *repressed, unconscious triggers* to which he or she is adapting outside of awareness. On this level, both the stimulus (trigger) and response (unconscious processing) are *unknown to the patient*, even as these processes move forward. The therapist's engagement in decoding disguised narrative images in light of their triggers is known as *trigger-decoding*. It is the only known means by which deeply unconscious adaptations can be ascertained.

## RETURNING TO THE VIGNETTE—
## MANIFEST CONTENTS

Chapter 2 initiated our clinical pursuits with a brief clinical vignette. Let us return to it now in light of the perspectives we have been developing.

The excerpt was one in which the therapist had not as yet intervened, so all we can do for the moment is examine and formulate the material from the patient—beginning, as always, with the surface, the manifest contents. The *conscious adaptive issue or trigger* for Ms Allen was constituted by seeing her hostile and seductive uncle at a family gathering. The uncle's presence was experienced as a threat (a source of activating danger and anxiety), and the patient's conscious coping response was to keep her distance from him.

At the same time, the immediate experience stirred up a number of disturbing conscious memories about the uncle, some of them directly involving Ms Allen. There are indications that the anxiety evoked by these recollections activated some conscious processing or working over of the earlier experiences, evidently designed to reduce their potential to disturb the patient.

While all of this is emotionally charged, it is quite unremarkable—adapting to a meeting with a threatening figure by avoiding him and working over the recollections the experience aroused seems quite reasonable. There is, however, something too straightforward and simple to the entire process, and it seems to lack the complexity, nuance, and depth we would expect in dealing with emotionally charged issues. This analysis also speaks for a very simple, one-system design of the emotion-processing mind; it merely indicates that we have a conscious intelligence for adapting directly to known emotionally charged triggers and the memories that they arouse. In some situations, this may well be all that is needed, but it is quite likely that these surface events also mask a deeper and stronger adaptive issue. We will keep this possibility in mind as we proceed.

As this point, some therapists might want to turn to psychoanalytic theory and suggest that there is more than meets the eye in Ms Allen's associations. They would argue that the material contains a host of *implied meanings*, many of them outside of the patient's awareness—i.e. unconscious. However, the purported nature of these unconscious communications and their implications would vary greatly depending on the proponent's theoretical bias.

Some therapists would propose that the patient had had an unconscious sexual attraction to her uncle and that these wishes were projected onto the uncle. Others would argue that the uncle represents the patient's father or brother, and that her own incestuous desires and conflicts are reflected in the dream—ergo her difficulties with men. Still others would invoke the concept of transference and suggest that, unconsciously, the patient wished to seduce her therapist and that she projected these feelings onto her uncle.

These somewhat arbitrary formulations—and there would be no means of validating any of them—again reflect the weak adaptive position. They imply efforts by the patient to cope with an adaptational issue, but *they do not define an immediate and specific adaptation-evoking trigger within the therapeutic interaction*. They propose a variety of intrapsychic conflicts within the patient rather than an unconscious response that has been triggered by a specific intervention by the therapist. They therefore defy the basic premise that states that the emotion-processing mind is designed to cope with contemporaneous environmental impingements; they lack a definitive adaptive cast. Furthermore, these formulations speak primarily of projection and fantasy, while the strong adaptive approach would speak of unconscious perception and the introjection of the qualities of real experiences, such as an intervention by the therapist, rather than projected fantasy.

The main point for us, however, is the realization that none of these formulations reveals much about the architecture of the mind. They speak mainly of mental mechanisms rather than mental structure, and of the dynamics of conscious and unconscious conflict rather than the design of the mind. To the extent that a design of the mind is suggested, the proposed configuration would essentially envision a single processing system for dealing with emotionally charged impingements, with components that operate both within and outside awareness—and with strong connections between the two. Essentially, the model would be that of a unitary emotion-processing mind with conscious and unconscious subsystems.

## FREUD'S TOPOGRAPHIC MODEL

The two models of the mind proposed by Freud (1900, 1923) are both of the single system variety. The first model, stated mainly in *The Interpretation of Dreams* (1900), is called *the picket-fence model* in that it proposes a series of sequential mental systems operating with and without awareness—a *UCS* (unconscious) system with strongly repressed mental contents; a *PCS* (preconscious) system with unconscious contents that are relatively easily brought in awareness; and a *CS* (conscious) system with both attention and awareness. The transition from one system to the next as contents move towards awareness involves a passage through a censorship or defensive barrier that must be overcome or modified in some fashion if UCS contents are to be made CS.

In presenting this model of the mind, Freud proposed that mental processing is activated by a stimulus (trigger) that obtains conscious registration before being shunted off into the unconscious part of the mind (UCS). Although he knew of Poetzl's experiments with subliminal perception, Freud never integrated unconscious registration into his models of the mind—a gap in clinical thinking that has, even in the face of extensive research into subliminal perception, remained with most therapists until the present time.

In considering Freud's models, it is well to reflect on his clinical writings as they reveal his ways of listening to, formulating, and interpreting the material from his patients. For Freud, resistance was virtually a conscious phenomenon. When he offered an interpretation (and he assumed it was inherently valid) and the patient objected or did not accept it (directly and consciously), Freud saw the patient as resisting. Many of the interpretations he offered similarly addressed manifest and conscious communications from his patients. Freud merely suggested implications to these communications of which he, but not the patient, was aware. Quite often these implications involved formulated transference fantasies and their unrecognized genetic sources. Freud did not adopt a strong adaptive position, nor did he trigger-decode his patients' thematic images in light of his own interventions.

Returning now to the workings of Freud's so-called *topographic model of the mind*, he proposed that dangerous or anxiety-provoking ideas move from consciousness into the unconscious system of the mind (UCS). Any effort to retrieve a repressed idea meets with a first line of censorship or defence that bars it from entering the PCS system. If a means such as disguise is found to enable the fantasy or wish—the types of contents Freud proposed for the unconscious mind—to move past this defence, it enters the PCS system where it is readily available to move into the CS system and enter awareness, a step that involves passing through another but lesser censorship. Once the idea enters the system CS, there is some kind of behavioural response—a motor discharge, as Freud termed it.

This model of the mind proposes a single psyche divided into three systems, an architecture of sequential repositories for repressed ideas. There is a processing sequence that moves the idea—the fantasy, memory, or wish—from one system to the next, a movement that depends largely on the status of the patient's mental defences and the nature of the repressed contents. The latter generally pertained to incestuous and other forbidden sexual wishes and, to some degree, to forbidden hostility or violence.

The system UCS was seen to be comprised mainly of repressed wishes and memories—it was the forerunner of the id (see below). The censorships are defensive and repressive formations, and the system CS was viewed as an executive system and as the locale of the conscience—it was the forerunner of the ego and superego.

For us, perhaps the most striking feature of this model of the mind is that it has an *interactional cast*—there is a stimulus, a sequence of mental processes, and a behavioural outcome. There was considerable potential for developing this model into one with a strong adaptational orientation (Langs, 1992b). But even if this lead was pursued, Freud was constrained by his overly intense focus on fantasy and the mind of the patient, and the patient's interactions with others outside therapy. Within therapy, the model was used to study the patient's processing of his or her repressed fantasies, wishes, and memories—the interactional and strongly adaptive aspects of the model were lost and with them a view of the mind as an organ for immediate coping.

## *FREUD'S STRUCTURAL MODEL*

Freud (1923) abandoned his topographic model when he observed that the defences that he had located in the conscious system often were unconscious—patients were often unaware of the resistances that he, as their analyst, believed were operating. CS defenses that are outside a patient's awareness belong in the system UCS. Given Freud's primary commitment to conflict theory and to intrapsychic and intersystemic conflicts as the basis of neurosis—the system UCS and its forbidden wishes pitted against the system CS and it defences—the model appeared to be seriously flawed in that the supposedly warring parties belonged to the same side or system rather than to opposing sides.

In addition, Freud realized that the conscience, which he had located in the CS system (i.e. conscious moral values), also operates in a largely unconscious fashion and must therefore be part of the system UCS. He came to this formulation because his patients often behaved in keeping with a need for punishment and were unaware that this was the case. Here, too, the model failed to be compatible with the conflict theory of neurosis, and revision was called for.

With so many internal inconsistencies, Freud eventually gave up this model of the mind and replaced it with *the structural model*, which posited three systems of a single mind, each with conscious and unconscious components—the ego, id, and superego. In abandoning the topographic model, Freud gained a great deal with his new design, but he gave up a great deal as well (Langs, 1992b).

First, the new model lost the interactional cast of the earlier model, and, thereby, considerations of interaction and immediate adaptation became even more peripheral than before in psychoanalytic thinking. Second, the new model was so simple and straightforward, so seemingly complete and useful, that there was virtually no remaining interest in model-making. The abandonment of efforts at mapping and modelling entailed a serious loss for psychoanalysis—the creation and revision of models that is vital to all sciences.

Third, the new model used a structure's *functions and capacities* as its main way of defining its three entities. The first model used *the state of mental contents—whether they were conscious or unconscious*—as its primary criterion for the definition of the systems of the mind. Secondarily, the nature of a system's contents and functions were called into play. In the new model, there were conscious and unconscious features to each of the systems of the mind, and this aspect no longer played a primary role in defining a system.

The main problem with the downgrading of the concepts of conscious and unconscious functioning, and the postulates of unconscious communication, experience, and systems of the mind, is that "the unconscious" stands as the basic cornerstone of psychoanalytic theory. The loss of criteria related to unconscious functioning can be thought of as a step away from the heart of psychoanalytic thinking.

To summarize, the structural model proposed by Freud divides a single psyche into three functional systems—ego, id, and superego. Each structure has conscious and unconscious components, and the main criterion for defining a system of the mind lies with its functions—the id houses the instinctual drives; the superego is the seat of the self, conscience, and ideals; and the ego embodies the executive and defensive capacities of the individual.

This revised model posits that the conflicts underlying neuroses lie within the mind of the patient in the form of intrapsychic conflict—issues that materialize between the systems of the mind (e.g. an inappropriate or forbidden id wish that the superego condemns and the ego defends against through repression). Recent attempts to consider interpersonal triggers for these conflicts in light of this model of the mind have done little to change the prevailing structural blueprint of the mind. These latter efforts merely stress the role of the ego in dealing with external reality and in mediating between reality and the three systems of the mind. Within therapy, this object relations position still focuses on the mind of the patient—and on his or her inner fantasies—though a weak nod is given to interventions by a therapist that sometimes activate these inner constellations of memory and fantasy. The focus remains on the experience of the patient in terms of fantasies and projections, and specific triggers and immediate adaptations within therapy are generally not considered.

All in all, the conventional forms of dynamic psychotherapy call forth a model of the mind that posits a single mental system that embodies a broadly defined set of interconnected conscious and unconscious structures and functions. There is conscious coping and unconscious influence. There are conscious and unconscious psychic defenses that guard against the awareness of conflicted, forbidden wishes and fantasies, and *repression*—being unaware of mental contents—is the fundamental defence.

The structural model per se was able to add little to our understanding of the therapeutic interaction, nor did it create—as it should have—any pressure from unsolved puzzles or anomalies (Kuhn, 1962) that might have led analysts to modify Freud's model or seek out viable alternatives. As a result, model-making was almost entirely abandoned—a great loss for the field in that, as noted, making and revising models of basic entities is an invaluable pursuit in all known sciences.

It seems clear now that it would take an entirely new way of observing and thinking about the therapeutic interaction to unearth the concealed, but inevitably present, inexplicable anomalies that define the limits of the explanatory powers of psychoanalytic theory and clinical practice. In turn, these unsolved puzzles would challenge Freud's models of the mind and create pressures to develop fresh models in the hope of generating solutions to these unexplained anomalies. Because it is a theory filled with "epicycles"—explanations designed to fill in all gaps in knowledge—psychoanalysis has the misfortune of being almost incapable of discovering the limitations of its own theory and clinical practices. This, too, results in the loss of much-needed motivation for change—including the quest for fresh models of the mind.

So, it is with a sense of dissatisfaction in the existing models of the mind and their general explanatory powers that we turn now to a search for a more incisively defined and viable alternative—a fresh view of the architecture of the emotion-processing mind.

CHAPTER FIVE

# The communicative-adaptational model of the mind

To this point, we have generated a variety of formulations of the material from our clinical vignette. Each line of thought stressed the intrapsychic operations of the human mind as observed within a globally conceptualized therapeutic interaction. We found that these formulations suggested a rather broad view of the design of the mind as being three interconnected systems—originally, UCS, PCS, and CS; later on, id, ego, and superego.

Something unexpected and almost magical occurs when we shift our way of observing and formulating into a mode that centres on *immediate adaptive responsiveness* in lieu of the vague and general (weak) adaptational approach characteristic of the standard viewpoints on psychotherapy. A major transformation takes place in our thinking and in our model of the mind. Let us see how this dramatic change comes about.

41

## *SOME FATEFUL OMISSIONS*

The description of the transactions of Ms Allen's therapy—the clinical material or observables I presented earlier—and the previously discussed formulations of her free-associations would satisfy most present-day therapists. There would be some debate over the most important implications of the patient's material, but the clinical data would not be found wanting.

While we seldom think much about it, clinicians who summarize a psychotherapy session—and even those who mistakenly blatantly violate a patient's and their own privacy and confidentiality by presenting a recorded session (the only viable exception to the nonrecording of sessions is the need to do so for quantitative research purposes)—are offering a generally accepted selection of observables. The practice of presenting material from a patient, with or without the therapist's interventions, is standard procedure these days. It is erroneously believed that the communicated material of a given session is sufficient data on which to develop a clinically valid and fully serviceable picture of the therapeutic interaction—and the design of the mind.

Communicative-adaptive studies have shown, however, that clinical material alone—even when it is based on sequential process notes that reflect the patient's free associations and the therapist's interventions—is *not* sufficient data on which to base a valid and comprehensive, fully explanatory picture of the therapeutic experience. These studies indicate that critical variables are omitted in this way and that we must expand our field of observables—and that doing so remarkably changes our picture of psychotherapy. Introducing these added areas of experience in our efforts to comprehend the therapeutic interaction will provide us with an impressive lesson in how one's field of observation compellingly affects one's view and understanding of nature—including psychotherapy.

What, then, is missing from this description of nature? What other important, and possibly critical, segments of nature—kinds of data—can be added to this selective report of the transactions of the session given in chapter two? There are several answers to this critical question.

First, there is no mention of *the setting and ground rules of the therapy—its frame*. Acceptance of this omission implies that the conditions of treatment are inert and irrelevant to the therapeutic experience and the process of cure. Yet everything we know about nature indicates that boundary conditions, frameworks, and contexts deeply affect the elements or entities that function within its confines. The nature of the ground rules of this therapy and its setting is essential information, and adding this information to our picture of the treatment experience will deeply affect—and revise—our thinking about Ms Allen's material, as well as our ideas about the overall transactions of this treatment experience. This void must be filled with descriptions of both the established *background framework* of the therapy and all *recent frame impingements*—whether interventions by the therapist or behaviours of the patient.

This brings us to the second omission, namely the absence of any reference to the recent interventions by Dr Barton, whatever their nature—especially those made in the previous session, as they are likely to be active issues for the patient in the present one. The omission of allusions to the current or recent interventions of a therapist reflects an assumption that the patient's psyche operates without immediate influence by the therapist—his or her silences and/or active interventions. This, too, is clearly an erroneous assumption in that we know full well that humans are interactional beings who are greatly affected by the immediate and recent words and actions of others—be they therapists or patients.

In the session I presented, Dr Barton had not as yet intervened. However, he had intervened in the previous session, and his comments in that hour had definitely set the stage for the present one. The patient was working over and adapting to the influence of these interventions, even though a week had passed since they were made. Indeed, as we will see, this kind of carry-over is typical of the unconscious mind and may occur consciously as well—though far less often.

There is, then, a gap in the presentation to this point in that there is no mention of *an adaptation-evoking trigger*—an intervention by the therapist that the patient is likely to be working over, consciously and especially unconsciously. Without knowledge of the patient's *immediate adaptive tasks*, and especially of the stimuli that she may well be dealing with outside of awareness, we are missing a vital dimension—the adaptive aspects—of this therapeutic moment. We also have no way of formulating this material in terms of active *unconscious* meaning as defined through encoded narrative responses to adaptation-evoking triggers.

While Freud's overriding focus on the workings of the mind of the patient had brought with it an array of insights, this concentration also served as a way of precluding a full and sensitive picture of the nature of the therapeutic interaction. Indeed, on the basis of the material offered, our formulations must, by virtue of the limitations of the data, be confined to the manifest contents of patients' free associations and their implications. An adaptation-oriented reading of this patient's conscious, and especially unconscious, responses to events within the therapy is simply not feasible without a presentation of the events to which she was reacting. And these exclusions would, as noted, confine us to a simplistic model of the mind.

## *FURTHER MISCONCEPTIONS*

It is analytic folklore to think of the ground rules of therapy as being established at the outset of treatment and then fading into the background of the therapy. The patient's material, isolated from the dynamic effects of the setting and frame, becomes the sole field of study and the context for the therapist's interventions. Clearly, this approach suffers from grave omissions and is essentially in error.

In addition, it is generally thought that a therapist's intervention is a valid offering unless it is discovered to be blatantly in error. Interventions are also seen as cognitive efforts at generating insight. The psychodynamic factors in a therapist's selection of interventions, as well as the influence of the patient's specific communications and the ground rules and setting, are all but ignored.

In this view, a patient is seen as responding largely to a therapist's manifest communications. The unconscious and encoded aspects of the therapist's efforts are afforded little, if any, credence or consideration. In this light, insight is thought of in coldly cognitive terms, and it, too, is isolated from the conditions of treatment and the deep nature of the communicative exchanges between patients and therapists.

The idea that the behaviours and verbalizations of a psychotherapist convey a wide range of *unconscious* meanings and have a vast number of *unconsciously transmitted* effects on the patient is little appreciated. The sense of the ongoing and powerful unconscious dialogue that transpires between the parties to therapy is blunted, and no effort is made to follow the fullness of this deep interaction from one moment to the next. Constrained observations lead to constrained and often erroneous formulations and theories.

The material to this point, then, has limited us to the weak adaptive viewpoint. Without triggers, there can be no trigger-decoding—no appreciation of the encoded, unconscious meanings of the patient's material. And if there is indeed a complex *unconscious adaptive processing system* in the human mind, we would have no way of observing its effects or formulating its operations. To do so, we would require the identification of the most compelling adaptation-evoking triggers or stimuli for the patient so that we could formulate her responsive free associations as displaced, disguised, and *encoded unconscious* responses to those trigger events.

In all, a therapist who fails to observe the many ramifications of his or her interventions, and who fails to monitor the state of the frame and to recognize frame-related interventions, operates in a world that is severely constricted by his or her limited vision. Such a therapist has no way of seeing many of the most powerful happenings within a therapy, events that have quite forceful and critical unconscious effects on both members of the therapeutic dyad—and on their state of mental health.

If we stop to think about it, this very gap in the observational field of most practising psychotherapists must itself be a reflection of the basic architecture of the mind—it is an almost universal attitude. *The human mind seems to be designed in some way to be blind to vital aspects of human emotional experience and communication.* Thus, even though we are for the moment only speculating, we can nevertheless sense something of the truly unprecedented ways of thinking that characterize the strong adaptive position.

## A COMMUNICATIVE–ADAPTIVE RECONSIDERATION

Let us return now to the clinical vignette we have been considering in order to fill in the missing pieces so we can see where they take us. We may begin this fresh foray by asking a question: what were the basic ground rules of this therapy and was there a current frame impingement or other intervention(s) made by Dr Barton that was serving as an active, adaptation-evoking trigger at the moment?

To answer: as for the base-line conditions of this therapy, Dr Barton worked in an unshared, private office in a professional building. At the outset of the therapy, he defined for Ms Allen a secured fixed frame related to time, fee, and responsibility for sessions (see chapter three), and he tried to work interpretively with his patient. Ms Allen had been referred to Dr Barton by her physician, and she paid the fee from her own earnings; relative anonymity and total privacy and confidentiality also were intact. Indeed, the background frame was quite well secured—a rarity in today's world of psychotherapy.

There was, however, an immediate frame impingement for the session that we are considering—an intervention of considerable importance. The session that we have been looking at took place on a legal holiday. The holiday had come soon after Dr Barton's summer vacation, so he decided to hold sessions rather than cancel them.

We have now identified a frame-related, *frame-deviant trigger*. It had not been mentioned manifestly by the patient, nor was it introduced by the therapist (indeed, to do so would bypass the patient's communicative defences; it would be an erroneous intervention). Nevertheless, we may ask to what extent and how does knowing about this trigger reshape our thinking about the session and Ms Allen's material?

Theoretically, based on extensive prior clinical experience (Langs, 1982, 1992a, 1993a), we would expect this frame alteration to pose a significant adaptive task for Ms Allen's mental processing systems. However, we must turn to the clinical material to determine empirically whether there is in actuality any convincing evidence that the patient was indeed working over and adapting to this frame-modifying intervention.

If we look first, as we should, at the patient's manifest material, we see that there is no direct mention of the fact that the session at hand was taking place on a legal holiday. In fact, the patient did not mention this oddity until the following session and then did so only to remark that the streets had been empty around the therapist's office after her previous hour, and that she had felt anxious and endangered at the time. Despite this belated reference to the holiday session, formulating the *manifest material* would *not* lead us to think about the ground rules of the therapy for very long—if at all—or, for that matter, about any other aspect of the frame.

The question, then, must be: is there evidence in her narrative free-associations that, despite her conscious disregard for this frame violation, Ms Allen was working over and adapting to the deviation on some *deeply unconscious* level? That is, is this trigger, which evidently has been *repressed* for the moment, *represented or portrayed in disguised or encoded fashion*—and does her imagery organize meaningfully as an encoded response to this same trigger event? This is tantamount to asking whether the human mind is designed so that it copes with certain types of trigger experiences entirely without awareness. An affirmative answer would suggest that we have two, rather than one, emotion-processing systems of the mind.

In observing and formulating the events or communications within a therapy situation, we are unaccustomed to searching for and identifying *encoded representations of triggers*. Nevertheless, especially stressful triggers (and they often involve frame alterations) are often repressed and go unmentioned by the patients who experience them—and the therapists who are responsible for them as well.

On the other hand, should this kind of traumatic trigger be alluded to directly, patients often then will heavily disguise their encoded responses. In addition, triggers are almost always kept quite separate from the encoded images that reveal the patient's unconscious experience and processing of the triggering intervention. As we will see, *splitting off a trigger from the encoded themes that reveal its unconscious meanings* is the single most common and powerful *communicative defence* employed by the human mind.

## REFORMULATING THE SESSION

To return now to the question before us, is there a clear and unmistakable *encoded representation* of the therapist's frame alteration—holding a session on a legal holiday? This intervention would be experienced as frame-deviant by all patients, regardless of whether or not the therapist had stated explicitly that he would not hold sessions on legal holidays. Doing so is universally experienced as frame-altering by the *unconscious mind*, though it happens that in this situation Dr Barton had indicated at the outset of the therapy that, by and large, he did not work on legal holidays.

Looking at the material from Ms Allen, it appears that there are two unmistakable encoded representations of this frame-deviant trigger. The first is the allusion to her uncle, who worked on Sundays and holidays, while the second is the reference to her own error in making the appointment with the author with whom she was working.

In each of these *displaced and encoded* allusions (and notice that one of them takes the form of an actual behaviour by the patient), there are clear *bridging themes* that extend from the manifest narrative image to the latent trigger—working on holidays and Sundays in the first instance, and making an erroneous appointment on a Sunday in the second case. There is, then, strong evidence that *unconsciously* this patient was responding to the unusual circumstances of having a session on a legal holiday.

There is more still. The patient's material can be organized around this frame-deviant trigger event, and the themes in Ms Allen's narratives can be read out as a responsive adaptive statement. The narrative indicates that the patient unconsciously experienced a number of different meanings in this action, and that, in processing these meanings, she responded to her subliminal perceptions with suggestions for how to cope properly with the trigger. These adaptive proposals are called *correctives or models of rectification*—they are only rarely offered consciously, but they are quite common in unconscious reactions to deviant triggers.

I call these proposals *suggestions* because, as we will see, Ms Allen did not take up and act on her own unconscious adaptive recommendations. Even as she took strong exception to the timing of the session, she came to the hour without protest. Here, too, we have a clue to the design of the mind—unconscious wisdom that goes unapplied in reality. Once more, we come upon a quite surprising proposition.

What, then, was Ms Allen's unconscious experience of the frame-deviant trigger? The imagery, trigger-decoded in sequence, says that it was perceived as forcefully seductive, entrapping, rapacious, and incestuous. It was also seen unconsciously as an act of violence and obscenely seductive, as well as an abandonment of Dr Barton's therapeutic responsibilities to his patient—and as a sign that Dr Barton was more concerned with earning money than he was with caring properly for his patient.

There is, as noted, a model of rectification—a suggestion that the frame be resecured—in Ms Allen's advice to her uncle that he should have spent more time with his family rather than working on holidays. This is an encoded adaptive suggestion to the therapist. To back it up, the patient adds the encoded point that holiday sessions promote addictive behaviours and pathology in those on whom they are forced—the allusion of the harmful effects of the uncle's work schedule on his daughter.

To continue the decoding and linking process: the incident at work—the patient's own lapse—encodes a perception of the deviation as a blatant error that was hurtful to the therapist himself and to Ms Allen and, again, as a seductive act. There follows an offer of an *unconscious interpretation* to the therapist that he may be forcing himself on the patient as a way of getting her to distance herself from him (a possible hint at thoughts of terminating the therapy) because of seductive feelings that he has towards Ms Allen.

Let us summarize what we have put together through trigger-decoding to this point, doing so with thoughts of how this analysis of the vignette reflects on the architecture of the mind. A frame-deviation by a therapist received no *conscious* attention whatsoever, yet it was worked over—adapted to—in some detail outside of awareness, *unconsciously*. This suggests a distinct split in the emotion-processing mind that begins at the *perceptual level*—conscious insensitivity (blindness) versus clear unconscious perception (vision).

It appears, then, that there are two rather separate and distinctive emotion-processing systems—one connected to awareness and operating quite defensively, and the other functioning outside of awareness and doing so with a sensitivity that suggests relative nondefensiveness. Clearly, the more effective system is the one that is operating unconsciously, even though the results of its processing activities do not reach awareness directly—they do so only in encoded form and without notable effect on the patient's immediate behaviours.

Notice again that the introduction of the strong adaptive viewpoint and of trigger-decoding reveals aspects of the emotion-processing mind that were impossible to discern using the standard way of observing and thinking about psychotherapy. On a practical level, it is quite apparent that a therapist's comprehension of the therapeutic interaction and his or her formulation of the meanings of a patient's material is radically different depending on whether or not trigger-decoding is invoked. Our picture of the architecture of the mind depends on these same factors.

Our sensory apparatus and our mental cognitive capacities have distinct limitations. Much of nature is invisible to the naked eye and ear. Similarly, many of the transactions and meanings that are experienced within a therapeutic interaction are unavailable to direct observation or simplistic formulations.

The human mind itself is immaterial and not open to direct observation. Therefore, we must gather our impressions of its structure and functions through indirect evidence such as studies of the behaviours and communications generated by that mind. The basic design of the mind must then be inferred on a similar basis. The results of these efforts, when they are cast in adaptive and interactional terms, are, as we have seen, quite unexpected—they appear to tell us a great deal about psychotherapy that we had not known previously.

For example, these fresh findings indicate that because of the division or split in the emotion-processing mind into two relatively separate systems, each with its own defences and intelligence, a therapist will intervene one way when he or she is addressing conscious-system experience and quite another way when attending to deep unconscious experience. In practical terms, he or she will work one way when the patient's material is being trigger-decoded and linked to the thematic images, and will intervene very differently when only the manifest contents and their implications are being addressed—without trigger-decoding. Because the deep unconscious system of the mind is the system that is sensitive to the ground rules of therapy, the importance and many effects of the frame can be realized only through trigger-decoding (Langs, 1981). How we do psychotherapy and how we envision the working design of the mind both depend very much on how we approach the substance of the therapeutic interaction.

Trigger-decoding has given us fresh eyes, and a vision of the emotional world that does not materialize without attention to immediate emotional stimuli and unconscious adaptive efforts as reflected in encoded narratives. As a result, we are now on the trail of an expanded and revised picture of the design of the emotion-processing mind. We will continue this pursuit in the next chapter.

CHAPTER SIX

# Some features of the emotion-processing mind

Our first foray into the design of the mind suggests that there are two rather distinctive systems of the emotion-processing mind—one that is linked to awareness, and another that operates entirely without access to conscious experience. Since this initial impression will be borne out as we proceed, we may now name these two systems of the mind. The first is called *the conscious system* and the second *the deep unconscious system*.

Let us turn now to another clinical situation for some further material through which we may begin to generate a well-defined map of the mind and further appreciate what this blueprint tells us about the therapeutic interaction and its techniques.

Gary Nelson, a young man of 17, was in once-weekly psychotherapy with Dr Adams, a woman psychiatrist. He sought therapy because he was doing poorly in school despite his high IQ. Gary was an only child whose parents had a stormy marriage.

The referral came from a school psychologist and the frame was secured, except for the fact that the parents paid for the sessions. Gary made the initial contact with Dr Adams himself, and the therapist did not see the parents.

About two months into the therapy, Gary began a session by handing a cheque from his parents to Dr Adams for the previous month's sessions. He then went on to describe a violent quarrel with his parents over his allowance, which he felt his parents use to control and manipulate him. They gave him different amounts of money each week depending on how well they thought he had behaved. Gary felt that they should be consistent in what they give him, but he would prefer their allowing him to live on some money he had been given by his grandparents—a suggestion they refused to consider, saying that the money was earmarked for his college education. Gary objected and felt that having to depend on them for money placed him in a horrendously vulnerable position where his parents had too much power over his life outside the family—and inside it too.

The turmoil at home was so intense that the parents began to question the value of the therapy and threatened to take Gary out of treatment. Dr Adams responded to this material and to the threat of termination by asking Gary how he felt about her seeing his parents, assuring him that he could be present for the meeting. A session with them might well be the only way to bring some peace to the family, she added. Gary thought a moment and then said that he had no problem with that idea—it might do his parents some good to talk to Dr Adams.

In the little time left in that session, Gary spoke of a friend at school whose parents had taken in a boarder. The situation at their home was now out of control. At first, the friend was uncomfortable when he, his mother, his father, and the boarder were at the dinner table together; something didn't seem right about it. Then there was an incident in which he thought he saw his mother kissing this man, and, later on, he found out that she was having an affair with him right under his father's nose. "Now there's something a mother shouldn't do", Gary added, "It just shows you how little you can trust your parents."

## FORMULATING THE SESSION

Let us pause to process the material in this excerpt to this point, again doing so with an eye towards the architecture of the mind.

We may quickly note that the weak adaptive approaches to this material would focus on the image of the unfaithful mother, and translate its seeming unconscious implications into an unconscious transference fantasy of a sexual liaison with the therapist, based on an unconscious incestuous wish towards the mother. Others would see the story as a reflection of an empathic failure by the mother. More rarely, in a formulation that gingerly approaches the interactive viewpoint, some therapists might suspect an empathic failure by Dr Adams but would not trace it to the proposed frame modification, which would be thought of, in conscious terms, as an empathic move. Still another assessment, couched more in terms of object relations, would see the patient having a transference fantasy aroused by the therapist through some verbalized intervention; here, too, the proposal to see the parents would not be appreciated for its many unconscious ramifications. These formulations are in keeping with the structural model of the mind in terms of id, ego, and superego, and that of a single mental system divided by a wide repressive barrier into conscious and unconscious functions.

I have, however, tried to present evidence and arguments that support the proposition that the human mind has evolved in a manner similar to all of the other organs of the body, primarily to adapt to its environment—physical, social, and individual. Coping reactions to conscious and unconscious perceptions, and to one's own behavioural and fantasied responses to environmental impingements, are secondary issues.

In this light, we are obliged to begin our analysis of this material with an appreciation of the most compelling adaptation-evoking trigger with which Gary was dealing in his psychotherapy. In this case, the trigger is manifest in the session at hand and self-evident—it is the therapist's proposal to have a session with the patient's parents. This is, of course, a *frame deviation* in that it departs from the ground rule that assures the patient total privacy and confidentiality for the duration of a psychotherapy—a ground rule that is also highly vulnerable to further alterations during the session with the parents.

While the main trigger is, then, the frame-deviant proposal made by Dr Adams, it is well to clarify an important aspect of how this error came about. In the session at hand, the material that prompted the therapist's suggestion involved a series of quarrels that the patient was having with his parents regarding his allowance. This problem is a conscious and real area of contention between Gary and his parents, *but its communication within the session indicates that the narrative carries unconscious, encoded meaning that bears on a prior intervention of the therapist*. It also means that the very quarrel that has overcome this family is based to a significant degree *on an unconscious issue related to Gary's psychotherapy*.

The central theme of the quarrel bridges over to the therapy and reveals the nature of the trigger that unconsciously is at issue—the fact that the therapist accepts payment from the patient's parents instead of Gary himself. Notice that the issue must be stated in trigger terms first before turning to the patient-indicator side. That is, the trigger is the therapist's accepting payment from the parents, while the indicator is that the patient pays his fee that way and not with his own funds.

We must, of course, acknowledge that in reality, in most cases, parents must pay for the therapy of their adolescent children who do not have funds of their own. To resolve this often misunderstood problem, it is necessary to develop a number of clarifying points. First, nature is nature, and a frame deviation is a frame deviation, no matter how compelling the realities on which it is based. The conscious system may try to rationalize away an existing or proposed departure from the ideal frame or deny its impact on all concerned, but the deep unconscious system will never do so—its encoded messages are quite clear about what is happening and its consequences.

Every frame alteration promotes a constellation of unconscious experiences with negative qualities, regardless of the basis for the departure from the ideal frame—a compromised hold and container is experience as such regardless of its basis. In addition, the deep unconscious system does have a capacity for perspective, so it will bring to bear modulating contingencies when they exist. These qualifying factors may diminish the traumatic aspects of the deviant frame, but they do not eliminate them. The loss of privacy—paying the fee brings the parents into the treatment situation—has detrimental effects on both the patient and the therapist. Some of these costs are reflected in the patient's narrative material, which points to not being in control of one's life and being open to undue influence because of the fee arrangement.

Many adolescents can find sufficient employment to pay for their own therapy. Failing that, they can often contribute some money towards the fee and/or open their own bank account so that they can give the therapist their own personal cheque—thereby minimizing the parents' presence in the sessions. In Gary's case, he had some money of his own, but he did not suggest, as he could have, that he use it to pay for his therapy.

Careful trigger-decoding and frame-securing therapeutic work with his material, including the images in this session, would soon lead Gary to appreciate his own unconscious frame-securing corrective—that he should be paying for treatment on his own. At the very least, the strong unconscious impact of the fee arrangement on Gary (and his parents) could be worked over and interpreted—thereby lessening its evocation of unconscious guilt and its broad toxicity for everyone. Without an appreciation of the strength of this trigger, however, the unconsciously wrought damage caused by this frame alteration would continue unabated.

We can be quite certain that the fee arrangement for the therapy was unconsciously fuelling the quarrel between the parents and their son. It is an unresolved frame issue in which all of the members of the family—and the therapist—are participating. Frame deviations evoke unconscious guilt and destructive, intrusive, and seductive unconscious perceptions; they are the main cause of many disruptive interactions and inner states. The uninterpreted and unrectified frame alteration is a traumatic trigger that was causing considerable disequilibrium in Gary's family. Frame modifications in a psychotherapy are the hidden cause of many dysfunctional interactions and symptoms in the patients—and therapists—who are party to them.

As for the psychotherapy situation, it was the therapist's failure to trigger-decode her patient's narrative material in light of the trigger of her accepting a cheque from Gary's parents that set the stage for her deviant proposal. A large number of frame deviations are invoked on this basis. There is a failure to trigger-decode the patient's material and bring into conscious awareness the unconscious experiences at issue. Typically, this error creates *unconscious guilt* in the therapist and other disruptive kinds of unconscious experience.

These effects tend to lead to efforts by a therapist to cope with his or her disruptive self-perceptions and the patient's negatively-toned unconscious perceptions through some kind of frame-altering enactment. In this instance, Dr Adams' decision may well have been based largely on unconscious guilt and a need to behave in a manner that would provoke some type of self-harm or punishment for the therapist herself—possibly in the form of the patient's terminating his therapy.

With regard to the architecture of the mind, this analysis gives us our first hints that *deep unconscious fear and guilt* have enormous power as determinants of emotionally charged decisions. This stands in stark contrast to our realization, made in the previous chapter, that *deep unconscious wisdom* has little say in what we do adaptively on the conscious level where life counts. This unexpected configuration will soon be clarified in some detail.

## CONSCIOUS AND UNCONSCIOUS EXPERIENCE

Instead of trigger-decoding her patient's material, including his model of rectification (that he should use his own money to pay his fee), the therapist enacted a frame deviation. This then became the major trigger for the patient's subsequent associations, which began with *conscious acceptance* and moved on to a narrative story that, not surprisingly, encodes the patient's *unconscious repudiation* of the same trigger. That is, on the surface, Gary perceived the idea of the therapist seeing his parents as a helpful act. However, the implications of this same trigger as experienced unconsciously were quite a different matter. Let us examine this unconscious response in some detail.

The story that Gary told alludes to a boarder. It seems clear that this image encodes or represents his unconscious perception of his parents' intrusion into his therapeutic space in light of the two triggers that are active at the moment: (1) the therapist's acceptance of the parents' cheque at the beginning of the session, and (2) the fresh trigger of the therapist's proposal to see the parents. As we formulate the subsequent images in terms of this latter trigger, we should realize that, through *condensation*, they apply equally well to the cheque-related trigger—both triggers involve invitations to the parents to come into the treatment situation.

We have initiated the process of trigger-decoding by identifying recognizable implications of the trigger event. We do so in order to be prepared to meet the encoded images and their themes half-way—the themes reflect unconscious perceptions of the main unconscious implications of the trigger. Still, even as we prepare ourselves for particular meanings, we must remain open to what may have been missed—conscious-system defensiveness must be safeguarded against during every step of this process.

In turning for the moment to Gary's *unconscious* response to the trigger event of the therapist seeing his parents, we should realize again that a patient cannot state directly a reaction of which he is entirely unaware. Instead, the human mind has been designed with a capability of conveying these unconscious experiences through stories and narratives that encode or disguise the unconscious response—the patient's subliminal perceptions of the trigger and its implications, and the unconscious adaptive considerations that have materialized through the processing of the trigger outside of awareness, including models of rectification.

Clinically, a patient will often first state his or her conscious reaction to a trigger (here, Gary's approval of the deviation). But then he or she is likely to shift to a narrative of some kind about some other topic or person. The patient does not, of course, realize that he or she has automatically done so as a means of revealing his or her unconscious reaction to the trigger event which seems to have been set aside. The shift from single-message, direct expression to double-message unconscious communication is not deliberate or conscious, but automatic and unconscious. Every frame-related trigger will evoke a narrative response in a patient, one that characterizes his or her unconscious experience of that trigger. *Communicating encoded responses to frame-related triggers is a fundamental psychobiological function that is basic to the architecture and functioning of the emotion-processing mind.*

When reacting to a frame-related trigger, sooner or later patients automatically shift into the narrative mode. This is their way of generating *displaced and encoded* images that convey their unconscious experience and processing efforts. Manifestly, they will move away from the therapeutic situation and tell a tale of some sort, usually of a personal nature, but latently the story encodes an unconscious reaction to that trigger.

In this case, Gary is, of course, quite aware of the trigger—it was mentioned just moments before he told the story about his friend's mother. What he does not know, however, are the implications of the trigger event that he is experiencing outside of awareness. He will tell his story believing that it has nothing to do with the intervention that the therapist has just made—a viewpoint shared by standard-model psychotherapists. In this way, Gary will maintain a split between the trigger and his encoded themes or perceptions. This is, as I said, the mind's primary defence against comprehending unconscious experience when a trigger is known.

Looking at the material from Gary, we see that *manifestly* he is associating to the theme of *parents* which had just came up, rather than to his therapist's *modification of the frame* which came up at the same time. He also has moved away, in the material, from his own parents to those of a friend. But there is compelling evidence that the new story is displaced from the therapist and therapy (as it no doubt is from Gary's parents, which is a secondary issue at the moment). The themes of this story *bridge* readily from the manifest narrative to the underlying trigger—the story is about frame-breaking, inappropriate alliances, third-party intruders, and betrayal.

With respect to the design of the mind, we should note that the observation that this patient immediately went to an encoded narrative fraught with unconscious meaning indicates that the deep unconscious processing system has a capacity to unconsciously perceive and work over incoming emotionally charged triggers with *great rapidity and evidently with considerable perspicacity*. The conscious response was immediate as well, though it was brief and constricted. In many cases, the direct reaction is entirely absent, even as the deep unconscious processing moves forward. What, then, was Gary's unconscious reaction to this trigger event?

The main *power themes* of Gary's story are those of intruding upon and/or seeing an inappropriate physical contact involving a mother and a man, and an affair between a mother and a boarder—between two people living together—for whom a sexual liaison is inappropriate. There is as well the theme of mistrust and an important model of rectification—a good mother (therapist) does not get involved with outsiders to her marriage (therapy).

This patient—as is true of all of us—is clearly of two minds. His response to this trigger is *not* unified and integrated, nor is there evidence of a single repressed reaction that simply needs to be brought into his awareness. Instead, there appear to be two separate, distinctive reactions—a conscious endorsement and an unconscious condemnation. In addition, the *manifest/conscious reactions are quite constricted and without much power* ("Sure, go ahead and do it"), while *the unconscious adaptive response is extensive and rather strong* (it touches on experiences of intruders, forbidden involvements, betrayal, and sexual and voyeuristic elements, and it adds a corrective). The unconscious reactions also entail the use of *condensation*—where the conscious response is singly focused, the unconscious reaction is at least doubly focused. The two systems of the mind appear to not only have different views of the emotional world, but also to operate, process, and cope in very different ways as well. At first glance, too, unconscious processing seems to have many advantages over conscious processing.

## SOME DESIGN FEATURES OF THE MIND

These observations, which are supported again and again in therapy sessions all over the Western world, appear to indicate the following:

1. There are two distinctive systems of the emotion-processing mind—one operating within awareness (*the conscious system*), the other doing so entirely outside awareness (*the deep unconscious system*).
2. Each system acts independently of the other.
3. The two systems operate quite differently with regard to perceiving, processing, communicating, and adapting.
4. The conscious system seems to be capable of working over only one trigger at a time, while the deep unconscious system appears to process several triggers simultaneously and to be able to create multiple-message, narrative vehicles that express the results of the system's adaptive efforts.
5. By and large, the two systems have diametrically opposite attitudes towards ground rules and frames—the conscious system favouring frame modifications, the deep unconscious system favouring frame-securing.
6. The conscious system appears to be restricted in perceiving the implications of emotionally charged and frame-related triggers, pallid in its grasp of the meanings of these implications, and limited in its response repertoire—indications that there is considerable defensiveness in the midst of its adaptive efforts.
7. In contrast, the deep unconscious system appears to appreciate a wide range of implications to the triggering interventions by therapists and is able to recognize and process the emotionally strong implications of trigger events.

8. There are indications that the adaptive responses of the conscious system are unreliable guides to how a therapist should intervene with respect to both interpreting and managing the frame, while the deep unconscious reaction seems to be quite reliable for such purposes.
9. The needs, wishes, values, and attitudes of the conscious system towards the ground rules appear to be self-hurtful and self-defeating, while those of the deep unconscious system seem to be highly constructive.
10. The behavioural response to an emotionally charged trigger—the actual adaptive reaction—seems to be governed by conscious-system processing, attitudes, and needs that are under the sway of deep unconscious fear and guilt. Deep unconscious system processing and intelligence or wisdom do not seem to affect these real-life responses.
11. While deep unconscious adaptive wisdom does not influence a patient's direct adaptive responses to triggers, it affects the patient indirectly via unconsciously driven after-effects. Thus, deeply unconscious appreciation for the hurtful aspects of a frame-deviant intervention will cause any number of adverse and symptomatic reactions in a patient.

## *AN ADDENDUM TO THE VIGNETTE*

These first impressions of the design and functional capacities of the emotion-processing mind—in particular, the last point—are further illustrated by what happened in this therapy after Dr Adams held the session with Gary and his parents. The consultation had dealt with their financial quarrel, as well as some of the other issues that had come up in Gary's therapy—most of them introduced in some general, nonspecific way by the therapist.

> Gary inadvertently missed the following session because he had somehow forgotten it. In the next session, after apologizing for his inadvertent absence and thanking the therapist for seeing his parents, Gary was inexplicably belligerent,

mistrustful, and argumentative with Dr Adams. The main story he told involved his relationship with his girlfriend, whom he had thought he could trust. He had been at her house, in her bedroom, earlier that week, and her parents were away. They began to fondle each other, when her girlfriend showed up and suggested that they make it a threesome. Although his girlfriend agreed, Gary found the idea quite repugnant; he got up and left.

Bringing another girl into bed with them was immoral, Gary argued. It would dirty and destroy the closeness between himself and his girlfriend. He decided to end the relationship, feeling that he could no longer trust her and that she was terrified of intimacy far more than he was.

It seems evident that the *interactional source* of (the *trigger* for) Gary's resistances—his missed session and attacks on the therapist—lay with the therapist's frame deviation of seeing the parents. Nevertheless, in the session, Gary once more expressed his conscious appreciation for this move—even though it was, as before, coupled with unconscious criticism. The therapist's frame deviation led to the patient's frame deviation—a common sequence in the therapeutic realm. Thus, this resistance seems to be both adaptive and maladaptive, in that Gary had sound reasons to stay away from his hurtful therapist, yet there are more effective ways of coping with this frame-deviant trauma than forgetting the hour—e.g. directly confronting the therapist regarding the issues and hurts caused by the consultation.

Given that Gary was unaware of the most critical source of his anger and distress, his unconscious perceptions of the therapist led him to an *essentially maladaptive-action form of discharge.* Only proper trigger-decoding of the story that followed the allusion to the parents' session, and a promise to rectify the frame by never seeing them again, could set this situation right and begin to restore the patient's trust in his errant therapist.

The unconsciously perceived fear of intimacy in this therapist and the valid unconscious experience of the session with the parents as a ménage-à-trois (all frame deviations are validly experienced unconsciously as sexually and aggressively charged) evoked a number of severely negative reactions in this patient. He fought again with his parents and uncharacteristically acted up when the principal of his school came into one of his classes as an observer. These over-reactions are additional maladaptive behavioural responses to the errant trigger, and they can be properly illuminated and worked through only with sound therapeutic efforts related to the therapist's frame alteration. There are many commonly unrecognized and unconsciously driven detrimental consequences of frame deviations.

We have developed a first glimpse of the architecture of the mind and the light it can shed on the techniques of psychotherapy. Much of what we have seen and formulated is quite unexpected. For example, respect for this design calls for a jaundiced view of patients' conscious reactions to therapists' interventions. Instead, the design suggests that the most reliable guide for both interpretive efforts and managing the ground rules of therapy lies with trigger-decoding a patient's unconscious responses to these endeavours.

The presence or absence of *encoded validation* appears to be the most reliable available guide to sound and unsound interventions. This means that the deep unconscious system rather than the conscious system offers the best possible advice regarding how therapists should behave and intervene. Because this guideline directs therapists in ways that run counter to conscious-system inclinations, it takes considerable effort—much of it directed towards overcoming seeming flaws in the design of the mind—to carry out truly sound psychotherapy.

We see more clearly now that a therapist who works with conscious-system confirmation, values, and directives is likely to be quite misguided and actually quite hurtful to his or her patients. On the other hand, a therapist who works with deep unconscious system confirmation, values, and directives is likely to be offering the patient a most sound form of treatment.

With this broad perspective established, let us turn now to a careful study of the conscious system of the emotion-processing mind.

*CHAPTER SEVEN*

# The conscious system of the mind

Our study of Gary's session suggested a number of aspects of the architecture and functioning of the emotion-processing mind. We had a glimpse of how the conscious system is designed and operates or adapts, and had a chance to compare some of its processing capabilities with those of the deep unconscious system. We want now to concentrate on the conscious system of the mind and to spell out its main structural and functional features. Excerpts from two additional therapy situations will help us in this task.

## AN INADVERTENT FRAME DEVIATION

Mrs Chase was in once-weekly empowered psychotherapy with Mr Hall, a social worker; she was severely depressed. Early in the treatment, Mr Hall came into the waiting-room to escort his patient into his consultation room and, as he did so, inadvertently brushed against her arm.

Once the session began, Mrs Chase reported a dream in which she was at a farm with a college girlfriend, Peggy. They are sitting on some hay in the barn and they are recalling and laughing about a hayride they had taken with their boyfriends when they were in college.

In associating to the dream, the patient recalled that Peggy's boyfriend came on to her on the hayride—he couldn't keep his hands off her. It was terribly inappropriate. Later she discovered that he had slept with many different women at school and was known as a reckless seducer of women.

Without going into detail, we may note that there were other narrative guided associations to this dream, embracing themes of seduction, rape, and incestuous sexual contact. Nevertheless, when she turned to searching for active triggers—and in particular, recent frame-related interventions by her therapist—Mrs Chase was quite blocked. She recognized that her themes were largely frame-deviant, but she could not think of a frame break by her therapist—or herself—that could account for (i.e. meaningfully link to) her imagery.

In time, and with much conscious effort, the patient did recall that she had recently been told by a friend that Mr Hall was married. This is a revelation by a third party that unconsciously is experienced by the patient as a self-revelation and modification in anonymity by the therapist. But Mrs Chase readily realized that this trigger was insufficient to account for the power images in her guided associations—in principle, every powerful theme in a narrative pool must be accounted for through a trigger that has implications in keeping with the meanings of the thematic imagery. The rule that there must be a frame-related active trigger to account for all power themes (i.e. sex; death, illness, and aggression; and unrealistic images) arises because a patient's narrative imagery always reflects his or her unconscious experience of a trigger—encoded images are almost never falsified or misleading.

Hearing that her therapist was married is primarily a self-revelation that would evoke themes of exposure, voyeurism, and revelation, and possibly the theme of seduction—all frame deviations have sexual and aggressive meanings. Nevertheless, the themes of rape and incest do not seem to fit easily into the meanings of the identified trigger. In addition, the thematic pool did not include allusions to third parties intruding into a relationship (a theme that would bridge over and relate to the fact that the information about the therapist came from a third party to the therapy and involved another third party as well—the therapist's wife).

In all, then, there were signs that Mrs Chase was repressing a critical trigger event and that this involved some kind of modification in the ground rules and frame of the therapy—the themes of rape and incest clearly are frame-deviant. Efforts at both *direct recall* and *allowing the themes to suggest triggers* had failed to modify her conscious-system repressive defenses.

At first, Mr Hall also was unable to identify the missing trigger event. He simply hoped that as his patient continued her pursuit of the key trigger, his own repressive barriers would be modified so that he could undo his blind spot.

When there are indications of an important missing trigger, the best strategy is to return to the origination narrative (here, the dream) for additional guided associations. The wisdom behind this approach lies with the finding that the deep unconscious system knows very well the identity of the missing trigger, even as the conscious system does not. But the deep unconscious system can speak only through disguised narratives; giving that system a voice through fresh guided associations is therefore the best means through which one can discover a repressed trigger—especially when conscious searching has failed to do so.

Through leading questions, Mr Hall led his patient to the realization that there seemed to be a missing trigger, and that more guided associations were needed.

> Mrs Chase returned to her dream and said that the barn recalled a time when she was accidentally kicked by a horse. On another occasion, she was visiting a girlfriend who lived on a farm. She had been in the barn with the friend's brother when he had touched her breasts. When she objected, he said it was an accident—he hadn't meant to do it.

This last image finally jarred Mr Hall's memory—though not Mrs Chase's. His conscious-system repression was finally modified *by virtue of the power of the thematic clues* in Mrs Chase's guided associations. He wondered how he could have forgotten the incident of brushing against his patient prior to the session—it was the kind of frame break he should have kept in mind as the session unfolded.

Mr Hall asked his patient to bring these last images into the process—i.e. to work with the themes as clues and bridges to the missing trigger. It took an enormous amount of effort and leading interventions by Mr Hall to enable Mrs Chase to get around finally to realizing that the images suggested that Mr Hall had modified the frame in some seductive and physical manner. Even then, she could not think of an incident that fitted with those themes, so she returned to her dream for another guided association. This time she recalled a teacher she and her friend Peggy had had in college. He had a sneaky habit of getting too close to his female students and touching their bodies.

As this point, Mrs Chase let out a laugh. She had finally modified her own exceedingly strong conscious-system, repressive barrier. She suddenly recognized the repetitive themes of inappropriate physical contact and remembered the incident of the physical contact between herself and her therapist immediately before the session.

### MODIFYING CONSCIOUS-SYSTEM REPRESSION

There are many ways to modify conscious-system repression. With regard to *repressed triggers*, in empowered psychotherapy the most common means is reflected in this vignette—the build-up of encoded thematic clues to a missing trigger until the images overwhelm the defence. More rarely, encoded clues to the psychodynamic issues underlying the experience of the trigger event help a patient to gain access to a repressed intervention of his or her therapist.

As for *repressed meanings*—i.e. situations in which the narrative pool is weak despite the presence of a strong trigger—the main way to modify conscious-system repression is for the patient to turn to the power themes in an origination narrative (usually, a manifest dream) and press for additional associations. Here, too, generating fresh guided associations is the main means of modifying the communicative defences of the conscious system. When the encoded images allude to the fear of discovery and/or meaning, interpretations of the patient's response to pressures from the therapist to move in that direction can be interpreted.

Returning to the vignette, once Mrs Chase had lighted upon the missing trigger, her first reaction to her realization was to deny that the incident had any meaning. She had forgotten it because it was so trivial, she argued. Here again, it took some definitive intervening by Mr Hall to enable Mrs Chase to bring together—link up—her power themes and the errant trigger. When she did so, she finally realized that while her conscious mind had dismissed the brush against her arm as insignificant, her deep unconscious mind had found a multiplicity of meanings—ranging from incest to a violent attack to all manner of inappropriate and secretly intentional kinds of physical contact.

The conscious system mobilizes very powerful denial and repressive defences in response to immediate and highly charged trigger experiences. The defensiveness of the conscious system of the mind in responding to emotionally charged events is amply demonstrated in this vignette. This defensive posture is, indeed, a basic and major property of the design and processing responses of this system of the mind—a surprising discovery about a system we have for too long taken for granted as committed to the search for meaning and insight.

## *ACUTE CRISES*

Some months later in this same therapy, Mrs Chase experienced the sudden death of her father. In that session, narrative material was sparse, triggers were elusive, and the bulk of the material involved conscious feelings about her loss. On leaving the session, Mrs Chase inadvertently stepped in front of a car, but fortunately at the last second she realized what was happening and was able to pull back, away from harm.

In times of acute emotional crisis and in emergency situations, the conscious system appears to take over the entire operation of the emotion-processing mind. Communicative responses are direct and with little, if any, encoded valence. The processing of the central emotionally overcharged trigger and of an acute danger is done manifestly and directly, with almost no sign of unconscious mental activity. And when the trauma has occurred in the everyday life of the patient, trigger events within the therapy will evoke only a minimal encoded response—one that is readily condensed with the sparse unconscious reaction to the outside disturbance.

It would appear, then, that in response to urgent and intense traumas, especially those that are death-related (see also chapter eleven), the conscious system takes over the workings and adaptations of the emotion-processing mind. Given that it is a system that is responsible for immediate and long-term survival, and is therefore especially responsive to emergencies and immediate, realistic dangers, this is not a surprising arrangement. The deep unconscious system shuts down so that all of the mental energies available to the individual are shunted to the conscious system of the mind. Even though its repertoire of adaptations is limited, they can nevertheless be focused and directed towards the danger situation to ensure an optimal response.

This arrangement suggests that evolution has favoured human minds that react to acute traumas, and especially those related to death or its threat, by obliterating, rather than facing, the activated emotional meanings of the trigger experience. This response often extends to a failure by the deep unconscious system of the mind to encode the unconsciously experienced implications of the unbearable realities for some time, especially when there is an immediate death-related trauma to adapt to. As more time elapses, encoded images usually begin to appear, but they are seldom spontaneously connected to the overwhelming trigger event.

Finally, we may take note of Mrs Chase's incident with the car. Stepping in front of the vehicle suggests the presence of unprocessed unconscious guilt and a need for self-harm, while pulling back from a car clearly reflects an emotionally charged, single-meaning, conscious-system, survival-related, adaptive action-oriented decision. This response is typical of the fundamental emergency survival-serving functions of this system, which extend into developing the means for long-term survival as well (see below).

## TRAUMATIC TRIGGERS

Let us look now at a therapy involving Ms Kelly, who was being treated by Dr Mines in a clinic setting. The patient had come into treatment for episodes of severe anxiety that had been evoked by the sudden loss of a job she had held for ten years.

> During the first two months of her therapy, there were a number of untoward incidents. On one occasion, Dr Mines found it necessary to delay her session by one hour and see her in another therapist's office because someone else was using the office in which he usually saw the patient. On another occasion, he missed a session because he overslept. At another time, he flew into a rage against the patient and severely reprimanded her when she missed two consecutive sessions, and several times he threatened to terminate the therapy unless Ms Kelly showed more rapid improvement. He also inadvertently dismissed the patient fifteen minutes early in still another session.
>
> In response to this unusual and extremely hurtful series of interventions, all of them frame-deviant, Ms Kelly (consciously) made repeated excuses for her therapist—he was overworked and exhausted; he had every right to chide her for not making faster progress; she really was a terrible patient; and none of this really was his fault, he was a victim of the chaos of the clinic.
>
> In contrast, Ms Kelly's narratives repeatedly touched on the

childhood abuse she had suffered at the hands of her long-suffering, deeply depressed mother and her violent, alcoholic father. Story after story detailed their abuse and insensitivity to her needs: their absence at her high-school graduation because her mother was immobilized by her depression and her father was drunk (a story she first told after the therapist had missed her session); their abuse when she got anything but a perfect grade (told after the therapist threatened to terminate her for not getting better faster); and not having her own room and having to sleep in the living room where she had no privacy (told after her session was delayed and moved to another therapist's office).

Ms. Kelly repeatedly complained that the harm that her parents had done to her was a major factor in her own tendency to get depressed. She never felt that her parents loved her, and she never knew where she stood with them—the only thing she could expect was the unexpected. Things would have been a lot better if her mother had left her father when he began to drink; instead, she just stayed around for more and more abuse. Talking about all of this was so depressing that Ms Kelly eventually asked if she could see Dr Mines twice instead of once weekly.

Consciously, this patient clung to and supported her therapist in the face of overt abuse. There was blatant denial of the hurts she had suffered, and she quickly forgot what had happened even a week earlier—signs of conscious-system repression at work again. She idealized her therapist and despite his repeated assaults asked to see him more often. Her behaviour and adaptive decisions regarding staying in therapy and wanting to increase the number of weekly sessions are in keeping with this conscious-system processing, even though the choices she was making look rather maladaptive in light of her therapist's abusiveness. There is, then, strong evidence of some kind of unconscious need in this patient for harm and perhaps punishment—such needs could well account for her staying in the therapy (see also below).

In developing a picture of the design of the conscious system, it is helpful to formulate briefly Ms Kelly's deep unconscious experience of these trigger events—this will serve as a critical means of comparison for conscious-system functioning. Where, then, does her deep unconscious system stand in all of this—how is that system processing these frame-deviant triggers, and what are its adaptive recommendations?

The patient made use of early recollections communicatively to convey her unconscious perceptions of her therapist's contemporaneous frame-modifying behaviours. These were, of course, the activating interventions that her deep unconscious system also was working over, although it did so *in terms of implications that were dramatically different from those alluded to and dealt with by the patient's conscious system.*

Story after story encoded the adaptation-evoking, frame-deviant, traumatic, and hurtful trigger events and the patient's unconscious perceptions of their harmful qualities. These images indicate that, unconsciously, Ms Kelly experienced Dr Mines' interventions as repetitions of the earlier traumas she had suffered at the hands of her parents. This was an accurate and realistic unconscious appraisal and not a matter of distortion and so-called transference. It is a valid unconscious experience of this therapeutic relationship for this patient.

Notice, too, that the very assaults that lie at the foundation of Ms Kelly's psychopathology are being recreated in her therapy by her therapist. Her deep unconscious system protests loudly against this tragic situation, but her conscious system endorses it and even asks for more of the same.

We are accustomed to think of this as masochism, the need for punishment, and to formulate such behaviour in terms of a repetition compulsion—a need to repeat the past in order to master it. But this does not account for why these behaviours defy the principle that nature and natural selection favour mechanisms that enhance survival. As we will see, whatever their psychodynamic sources, these behaviours also reflect the basic evolved architecture of the emotion-processing mind— one in which deep unconscious wisdom has little or nothing to say about our emotional adaptations, and deeply unconscious fear and guilt hold sway (see chapter 9). In any case, the self-defeating and self-hurtful aspects of the conscious system are quite evident here, as is its massive use of psychic defences in responding to emotionally charged triggers.

## SOME FEATURES OF THE CONSCIOUS SYSTEM

We have had a sampling of the conscious system in action. By adopting a strong adaptive viewpoint, and by *using the activities of the deep unconscious system as a basis for comparison*, we have been placed in a unique position to identify attributes of the conscious mind that could not previously be seen. On this basis, the following appear to be the main attributes of this front-line system of the emotion-processing mind.

1. *The conscious system is our basic survival-oriented system.*

The conscious system is designed first and foremost to ensure as much as possible an individual's immediate and long-term survival vis-à-vis environmental impingements and to satisfy the basic needs that sustain his or her existence. The conscious system is in charge of immediate adaptations, and it must, per force, be designed to cope rapidly and efficiently, and in a direct (manifest and single-meaning) manner, with life-threatening and other dangers (e.g. predators, harmful humans, physical threats to life and limb, etc.). It is also the system that negotiates social relationships and, ultimately, the mating experience and the generation of offspring—the survival of the gene and the species.

Given that the earliest hominids (humans) were not the strongest animals on earth, nor the fastest, their mental capacities evolved to provide them with a conscious intelligence that could outwit enemies and respond quickly and incisively—and without interference from other impingements—to physical and other danger situations. The conscious system also needed to have well-developed capacities and energies for securing food, shelter, companionship, and the like.

All in all, humans needed and need a clear and unencumbered conscious system, focused on manifest experience and its direct, nonsymbolic meanings. At times, this processing may be enhanced by limited amounts of affect and emotionally charged information, but the registration of overly intense affects or emotionally charged meanings would mainly interfere with these immediate adaptive efforts. This alignment seems necessary for both short- and long-term survival.

In general, physical dangers pose a far greater threat to life and limb than emotional dangers. Thus, we would expect that natural selection would favour individuals with strong conscious resources geared for prompt reactions to realistic dangers, and less so for coping with nonviolent emotional threats.

2. *On the whole, emotionally charged triggers or impingements, especially overly strong affects and meanings, tend to disrupt conscious-system functioning.*

While emotional impingements and arousal may, within limits, activate and enhance conscious adaptations (e.g. when one becomes frightened at the sight of an oncoming car), by and large emotionally charged impingements create adaptational needs that drain off the energies needed for conscious-system survival functions. Emotionally charged trigger events distract the conscious system from its main adaptive tasks and interfere with the system's coping skills and functions. In general, then, emotional issues tend to disturb direct adaptation (e.g. the hunter who is preoccupied about his wife's anger at him is especially vulnerable to predators; the woman who is worried about her husband not coming home the previous night is likely to mishandle her children or job the next day).

3. *With regard to emotionally charged events, then, the conscious system's primary response tends to be skewed towards self-preserving defensiveness.*

In order to safeguard its survival functions, the conscious system has been designed with a wide range of self-protective defences that are activated to reduce the disruptive impact of emotionally charged trigger events. There are *perceptual defences*, so that many of these stimuli are not experienced consciously at all—they are, by design, relegated to unconscious or subliminal perception. There is *conscious registration followed by denial* of the event and/or of its most compelling implications and meanings. And there is abundant use of *repression*—forgetting what has been experienced consciously. Communicatively, conscious-system thinking tends to be broad, non-specific, and clouded—ways of avoiding an incisive experience of specific exciting events and the well-defined, anxiety-provoking meanings they embody.

The human mind has evolved with abundant protection of the conscious system so that it may devote its energies to its survival functions. With so much to cope with in present-day life, the conscious system is relatively fragile and easily overtaxed. This helps to account for extremes of defensiveness vis-à-vis emotionally charged impingements that characterize the system. Contrary to standard model thinking, the conscious system is *not* geared towards a full appreciation of emotionally charged experiences; it does *not* favour deep unconscious insight (or the use of trigger-decoding); it does *not* deeply wish to experience unconscious meaning, even in disguise; and it also does *not* wish to comprehend the mind's unconscious perceptions and their ramifications. In the emotional domain, the conscious system tends to be a see-nothing, hear-nothing, know-nothing system.

Of course, the conscious system does not obliterate every emotionally charged trigger. However, it does repress or deny many implications of critical emotional impingements—clinical observation reveals a remarkable degree of conscious-system perceptual blindness.

When perceptual and repressive defences fail, the conscious mind automatically invokes a series of *communicative defences*—an emotionally charged trigger is recognized, but its most critical ramifications are repressed or denied; encoded stories are told but not recognized as conveying trigger-related unconscious meaning; and, above all, recognized triggers are not connected to the encoded thematic material that they have evoked, and no effort at trigger-decoding is made. These design features hold, of course, for both patients and therapists; thus, each in their own way should be committed in psychotherapy to overcome these tendencies and their ill effects.

4. *The conscious system has its own unconscious subsystem—the superficial unconscious subsystem.*

There is, of course, a reservoir of nonconscious memories readily available to awareness. The PCS system in Freud's (1900) first model of the mind is such a system, and in our terms this reservoir is an aspect of a *superficial unconscious subsystem.* This subsystem also contains memories, perceptions, and contents that are repressed—as reflected, much as we saw, in the forgetting and failure to recover *directly available (manifestly stated) memories of recent and past events.* (In contrast, deep unconscious system memories can be recovered *only in encoded form.*)

Another feature of the repressed contents within this subsystem is the ease with which they find manifest expression in disguised form. Where deep unconscious contents are extensively disguised, these more superficially repressed images are relatively transparent; often they take the form of well-known and self-evident symbols. A therapist's lateness to a session is portrayed through a teacher being late for class; a fee reduction is encoded as a sale at a store. This kind of imagery is lacking in power, and there is little sense of mystery or unexpected meaning when trigger-decoding is accomplished—the entire communicative constellation is patently self-evident despite the use of (minimal) disguise.

To cite a clinical example, after Dr Mines forgot Ms Kelly's session, she began the following hour with a series of (conscious) excuses for her therapist and with excessive forgiveness—a denial of the hurtful ramifications of this frame break. Ms Kelly then spoke of how forgetful her mother is, and of how often she would forget a date she had made and would leave the other person in the lurch.

The encoded image of the mother's forgetting an appointment readily decodes into the therapist's forgetting the session. There is no sense of deep experience, and nothing unexpected or convoluted is conveyed. This representation of one person's absence by another person's absence is the kind of repressed image and meaning that exists in the superficial unconscious subsystem. These repressed connections—here between the therapist and the patient's mother—tend to be self-evident and carry little in the way of emotional meaning. However valid it may be, the link between what is conscious and what is unconscious is so transparent and intellectualized, and so lacking in power, that this kind of decoding has few if any consequences for a patient's emotional life.

5. *With respect to ground rules and frames, the conscious system is frame-insensitive and inclined towards frame modifications rather than frame-securing efforts.*

As a rule, the conscious mind barely appreciates the enormous power that frame-related events have on patients and therapists, and on emotional life in general. A relative ignorance of the role and functions of ground rules and frames, and of frame-related interventions, is commonly shared by patients and therapists alike. This accounts for the looseness of attitudes towards, and the management of, ground rules and frames in virtually all forms of psychotherapy—except for those carried out by therapists committed to communicative/adaptive principles.

This disregard of the importance of frames is built into the architecture of the conscious system. This thesis is reflected in the clinical finding that it is usually very difficult to teach the conscious minds of both patients and therapists to think about and appreciate frames, and to structuralize frame-related insights so that they become part of one's conscious and direct adaptive armamentarium. There is, then, an *inherent* antagonism between frame-related ideas and conscious thinking.

6. *Many conscious-system behaviours and choices are motivated by unconsciously experienced death anxiety and guilt and, therefore, are self-defeating and self-hurtful.*

As is evident in these vignettes, and as we will see more clearly in chapter nine, conscious-system adaptations are *not* under the influence of the deep intelligence of the unconscious mind, but are unknowingly driven by deep unconscious fears (of death in particular) and guilt. This design feature appears to stem, on the one hand, from the inability of the conscious mind to tolerate in awareness the terrible meanings of the trigger events and their meanings that are processed by the deep unconscious wisdom subsystem, and, on the other, by the role played by unconscious fear and guilt in restraining the mind's natural inclinations towards violence, especially when a person is threatened or attacked.

7. *The conscious system is an extremely unreliable and dangerous guide to intervening and an untrustworthy source of validation for interventions.*

With respect to technique, it is well to realize that the very structure and functional design of the conscious system mitigates against using a patient's conscious advice or responses to interventions as a guide to one's therapeutic efforts. The system is far too defended, frame-insensitive, and inclined towards self-hurtful choices to be of much use to a psychotherapist with respect to determining valid and invalid interventions—verbal and frame-managing. This realization calls into question virtually every aspect of standard technique because these approaches have been fashioned through patients' conscious responses to therapists' interventions and, even more tellingly, by the conscious minds of psychotherapists without the benefit of trigger-decoding.

I must say that in developing a picture of the architecture of the mind, I found myself repeatedly surprised by how much I was learning about the conscious system and conscious functioning. As psychoanalysts and dynamic psychotherapists, we are so fixed on the pursuit of unconscious contents and effects, we hardly pay attention to conscious mental activities. The importance of appreciating the full design of the emotion-processing mind now makes it imperative that we adopt a more balanced approach—we need to know as much about conscious adaptive efforts as about deep unconscious adaptive efforts. To complete our picture of the mind, then, let us turn now to a more specific examination of the remarkable and little-known deep unconscious system of the emotion-processing mind.

CHAPTER EIGHT

# Probing the deep unconscious system of the mind

In Freud's (1923) structural model of the mind, there are unconscious aspects to each of the main structures—id, ego, and superego. In this model, "conscious" and "unconscious" become descriptive terms that have been downgraded to qualities of human mentation and experience; there are, as well, both conscious and unconscious structures and functions for each of the three components of the mind. Conscious and unconscious are no longer features that define or distinguish the systems of the mind. Thus, an id wish, an ego function, or a superego attitude could be within or outside awareness. The beacon light of psychoanalysis—*unconscious* mentation, experience, and communication—has lost its most of its power.

Current formulations of clinical material make use of a vague and global concept of an unconscious function, idea, or affect, and the term "unconscious" is used in a manner that is similar to the early uses of the terms "protoplasm" and "atmosphere". Both entities exist but were so ill-defined as to be virtually meaningless. Rather than serve science, these concepts retarded its advancement. So, too, with the current waste-basket employment of the term "unconscious" in psychoanalytic thinking—it interferes with the growth of psychoanalytic theory and supports poor and harmful clinical techniques.

## OBSERVING INTERACTIONALLY

As we have seen, this situation changes markedly when we adopt a strongly adaptational viewpoint. We are compelled to recognize that the emotion-processing mind is comprised of two distinct systems that are defined basically in terms of access and connection to awareness—*essentially in terms of conscious and unconscious structures and functions*. Conscious and unconscious experience, adapting, communicating, and the like critically define the design and capacities of the two systems of the mind—one essentially operates consciously, the other essentially unconsciously.

The strong adaptive position also facilitates a precise empirical definition of the terms "conscious" and "unconscious" which is not feasible with any other approach to these issues. The evidence for the existence of these two systems of the mind and the means by which we can fathom unconscious experience and communications are similarly well-defined.

*Unconscious communication* is reflected in encoded narrative messages that become sensible and yield deep and complex meaning only in light of an understanding of the fundamental adaptive functions of the emotion-processing mind. Technically, this brings us back to *trigger-decoding* as the prime (and perhaps, only) means through which we can define the deep unconscious realm. That is, unconscious experience is both concealed and revealed by narrative messages. In order to appreciate their encoded meanings, the narrative must be trigger-decoded so that the themes are linked to an active trigger in the form of an explanatory or interpretive reading of the disguised material.

Trigger-decoding shows us that in attempting to access unconscious communications, we do not engage in peeling away layers as is done in archaeological excavations but, instead, simply undo the camouflage and encoding that masks a second meaning in a surface narrative message. Technically, probing, exploring, and interpreting supposed implications of a patient's material that the patient seems unaware of is replaced by a build-up of narrative associational material, the discovery of the relevant evocative triggers, and a linking of the triggers to the themes extracted from these narratives to reveal the patient's unconscious experience of the trigger events.

Through these efforts, the existence of a distinctive and unique deep unconscious system of the emotion-processing mind is revealed. We have already seen its relative non-defensiveness and striking adaptive wisdom in the emotional domain. In this chapter, we develop a more detailed picture of the design of this system with regard to both its remarkable intelligence and its awesome fear/guilt subsystem, a system that has evolved with great power over human responsiveness and emotional life.

## A FRESH VIGNETTE

Mr. Drake was in empowered psychotherapy with Ms Brown, a social-worker therapist. He had sought therapy because of an inability to get his life going—he was unable to commit himself either to a lasting job or to a lasting relationship with a woman.

Some months into treatment, Mr Drake began a session with a dream in which he is in the living room of his apartment and hears a loud buzzing sound coming from his bedroom. He pursues the sound and finds a huge bee in the room; it begins to sting him and he wakes up.

Associating to the dream elements (i.e. invoking *guided associations*), Mr Drake thought of a newscast he had heard on the day of the dream which reported a story about a man who had accidentally stumbled into a beehive and was stung by hundreds of bees. Only quick medical attention had saved his life.

His bedroom recalled another apartment in which he had lived two years earlier. A thief had forced open a bedroom window and stolen his money and jewellery while he sat in the living room listening to music on his stereo.

We will by-pass the other guided associations that Mr Drake conjured up in response to these dream elements and turn to his pursuit of *self-indicators* (i.e. his own impingements on the frame of the therapy) and *triggers* (i.e. primarily the therapist's frame-related interventions). As for the former, Mr Drake "confessed" that he had given Ms Brown's name to a woman friend who was thinking of getting into therapy. He knew that it was wrong for him to do it, but he did it anyhow.

## *THREE LEVELS OF MEANING IN FRAMES*

This last communication reintroduces the ground rules or framework of psychotherapy. By giving a friend the name of his therapist and attempting to have her see his therapist, the patient has modified both the total privacy and total confidentiality of his treatment; he has compromised the security of the framework of his therapy. In order to discuss the implications of this frame modification, we must have a clear picture of the functions and ramifications of the ground rules of therapy.

In the remarkable and unfamiliar realm of *second unconscious experience* that is discovered through trigger-decoding—and it is distinctly different from the *world of conscious experience*—the world is organized in terms of ground rules, boundaries, settings, and other aspects of the frame. There is a *universal* set of attributes experienced by all humans in response to secured frames on the one hand and deviant frames on the other. This kind of consistency is a striking feature of unconscious experience.

In addition to these universals, there are two additional layers of meaning to all frame impingements. The first is a collection of *specific but also universal meanings that characterize a particular frame impingement*. For example, missing a session is a different frame deviation from that of overcharging a patient. They share the meanings common to all frame breaks—e.g. a failure in therapeutic holding and containing, a violation of the ideal ground rules, a hurtful act, a disregard for the patient's needs and welfare, and so forth. But they also have distinctive additional meanings that they do not share—e.g. the missed session is a sudden abandonment, while the overcharge is an act of greed.

The second added set of meanings of a particular frame impingement lies with its *personal valences for the patient and the therapist* who are involved in the transaction. For example, a patient with a history of early loss of close family members will be especially sensitive to a session missed by a therapist, and the activated genetic experiences may be overwhelmingly painful. In contrast, if the patient had been deprived emotionally and/or financially as a child, there would be an intense reaction to being overcharged by the therapist.

In all, then, in working through and attempting to detoxify and resolve the detrimental effects of a frame deviation, or in working through the death-related and other anxieties aroused by a frame-securing intervention, all three levels of meaning and experience must be dealt with as the patient's material permits. Indeed, the therapist should be on the alert for each of these aspects of a patient's experience of a frame impingement. The absence of material connected to any of these dimensions should be taken as a sign that the processing of the frame-related event has not been adequately carried out, and it is likely that the effects of the trigger event will extend into the following session.

It is important for both patients and therapists to become accustomed to organizing their worlds of deep unconscious experience in terms of whether a given event is frame-securing or frame-deviant. In addition, the specific ground rule that has been enforced or violated should be identified—an effort that runs counter to the conscious-system's defensive tendency to generalize and think in vague and uncertain terms.

In the conscious-system world, we have many organizers that we can turn to in order to deal with the incredible complexity of consciously experienced life—relatives versus friends; home versus work; helpful people versus those who are harmful; types of healers or merchants or professions or jobs; life versus death; etc. Clearly, the organizers are almost endless. Quite remarkably—and it is so unfamiliar to our conscious minds that we find it hard to believe—the deep unconscious system world is organized in much simpler fashion.

Evolution selected for unconscious minds that zeroed in on ground rules, boundaries, and frames as their prime concern. The inherent wisdom in this choice—i.e. its compatibility with nature as we understand it—lies with the previously alluded-to discovery that boundary and frame impingements are probably the single most powerful influence on all living (and non-living) systems and organisms. There is a remarkable economy of mental energies in this aspect of the architecture of the mind. How strange it is that the conscious mind finds this insight so difficult to accept (see below).

As for technique, these findings indicate that both patients and therapists must consistently identify and organize both self-indicators and triggers in terms of whether they are frame-securing or frame-deviant, or both. The latter is a not uncommon occurrence and refers, as a rule, to *modifying the frame in order to secure it better*. This occurs, for example, when a fee that is too low is raised to the therapist's usual fee.

## THE SECURED FRAME

In general, frame-securing implies strong holding and safety; the enhancement of ego functioning, a healthy superego, and a well-managed id; a positive self-image; clear interpersonal boundaries; thoughtfulness, delay of impulsive action, and insight; a healthy mode of relatedness; sanity; and reliable communication. This is an enormous package of positive features and effects. However, the secured frame is not without its sources of anxiety: it is a frame built on certainty, regularity, responsibility, and commitment. As such, the secured frame is confining and entrapping; it also creates a sense of separateness (however necessary and healthy) and vulnerability, and arouses death anxieties—life is encircled by death, and we are all entrapped in a claustrum from which the only exit is death. Nevertheless, the arousal of these persecutory, claustrophobic, and death anxieties within a secured frame creates the ideal conditions under which neurotic (or even psychotic) issues in these areas can insightfully be worked through.

When a frame is secured, then, there is the experience of both enhancement and anxiety. Regardless of who has secured the frame—patient or therapist—a patient's images will encode the positive aspects of the event and then shift to conveying the aroused anxieties. In addition to reflecting the constructive aspects of the frame-securing experience, these initial affirmative images serve to validate the trigger event—the frame-securing action or proposal.

Encoded validation of a frame-securing moment is an essential aspect of technique, in that it is needed to confirm the validity of the therapist's assessment of its positive effects and to make certain that the ground rule in question has been properly adhered to or rectified. Conscious-system deception is not uncommon in making these appraisals, and direct assessments cannot, generally, be trusted. The inclinations of the conscious mind are quite frame-deviant, and it is capable of conjuring up many rationalizations and attempts to justify any number of truly harmful frame-deviant interventions—including some that are invoked under the mistaken guise of securing the frame (e.g. inappropriately increasing a fee that is within a therapist's customary fee range because a patient complains that it is too low).

## *THE ALTERED FRAME*

What, then, of frame alterations? Departures from the *unconsciously sought* ideal frame are defined by negative and harmful *encoded* images generated in response to a proposed ground rule of a therapy or to any impingement on the conditions and rules of treatment. Frame deviations are universally experienced as harmful in various ways. They create pathological modes of relatedness between patient and therapist, and their invocation is a form of acting out—an attempt to resolve conflicts and anxieties by means of action-discharge in lieu of deep insight. Unconsciously, they are also perceived as acts of madness and as a reflection of a poor self-image and a disturbed identity, and as a consequence of ego, id, and superego dysfunctions.

Continuing the long list of detrimental effects, frame deviations are both assaultive and seductive, a means of achieving pathological forms of merger, and they enable patient and therapist to share pathological, interactional defences. In addition, such deviations create conditions of therapy under which communication is unreliable; they entail a contradiction between the inherent promise to be a sound therapist and the unsound ramifications of the frame break; and they create a disturbance in interpersonal boundaries with either too much or too little psychological—and, sometimes, physical—distance between the parties to therapy. They also afford all concerned inappropriate or pathological satisfactions.

In all, then, there are many ways in which frame modifications generate negative packages of harm and disturbance for both patient and therapist. Why, then, does the conscious system tend to seek out or sanction these hurtful departures from the ideal holding environment?

The answer lies in the enormously strong, however pathological, defensive and gratifying functions of frame deviations. Frame breaks provide unhealthy satisfactions and defences against deep anxieties, especially those that stem from experiencing a secured frame, such as personal death-related fears. Although often immediately expedient, frame deviations are harmful in the long run and cause much suffering to self and others. Still, the price paid for frame alterations often goes entirely unnoticed, and their negative consequences in the life of a patient (and therapist) are attributed to other causes—life's difficult, that was a bad break or someone else's fault, and so on. Seldom is it realized that personal harm is an inevitable consequence of all frame modifications.

Frame deviations tend to provide an individual with a false *unconscious* sense of denial of personal death in the sense that being able to break one rule is believed to imply that one can be the exception to all rules—especially the rule that states that death follows life. In addition, frame alterations provide denial and manic defences against the reasonable but threatening separateness and the feelings of helplessness inherent in the secured frame.

These two constellations of secured and altered frames organize unconscious experience, and they empower and guide the adaptive responses of the deep unconscious system. One set of coping responses is mobilized by secured frames, and quite another by altered frames. The deep unconscious vision of the two types of frames recognizes the positive aspects of secured frames and then experiences the anxieties they generate, while mainly stressing the dangers of an altered frame.

## CONTINUING THE VIGNETTE

We can return now to our vignette. Mr Drake had modified the ground rules of his therapy with regard to confidentiality (he had revealed his presence in the therapy), privacy (he had invited another person into his therapeutic space), and the one-to-one relationship (the friend was being asked into his treatment setting and would unconsciously be experienced as present in Mr Drake's therapy—this is the creation of a ménage-à-trois).

*Self-indicators*—mainly those that impinge on the framework of the treatment situation—serve several functions. First, they indicate where the patient stands with respect to his or her symptoms and resistances, and especially with respect to the state of the frame of the therapy. It is essential to know in each psychotherapy session whether a patient has acted to secure and/or modify an aspect of the ground rules of the therapy—the latter are, as I indicated, the major organizers of deeply unconscious life.

Second, given that the patient and the therapist together operate as a P/T system within a bipersonal field, the frame-related behaviours of the *patient* must reflect some aspect of the *therapist's* frame-related behaviours. In general, and with the exception of secured-frame, overly sensitive individuals, frame-securing efforts by therapists evoke frame-securing responses in their patients. On the other hand, frame modifications by therapists tend to evoke frame modifications by patients. It follows, then, that a patient's frame-related behaviours are clues to, and often a mirror image of, the frame-related behaviours of his or her therapist. In particular, a frame break by a patient calls for a thorough search for a similar intervention by the therapist. In all, then, self-indicators speak for both patient and therapist, and for disturbance or improvement in one or the other—most often, in both.

## THE SEARCH FOR A MISSING TRIGGER

The question with respect to our vignette, then, is this: what trigger event had activated this patient's decision to modify the frame? In light of the realization that the patient and therapist constitute a P/T system, this implies that we must seek the trigger for this self-indicator in some (probably frame-deviant) intervention by Ms Brown (we will engage in this pursuit with a mind open to detecting other, more unusual, possibilities).

Having identified his own frame-deviant self-indicator, Mr Drake began his search for active triggers in the hope of discovering one or more frame-related interventions by his therapist that had unconsciously evoked his frame modification. He concentrated his efforts at *direct, conscious recall* on the therapist's recent frame-management efforts and frame-related behaviours, and secondarily on other types of verbal comments such as interpretations, questions, and other kinds of interventions unrelated to the frame.

These latter interventions are called *impression triggers* because they are very difficult to define precisely, due to the complexity of verbal communication and the defensiveness and inherent uncertainties of conscious-system assessments. Given their relatively clear features, frame-related triggers tend to be far more easily defined (especially as frame-securing or frame-deviant). Thus, a patient's impression that a therapist had made a hostile, seductive, or otherwise inappropriate comment is open to a great deal of uncertainty, and it *must be validated unconsciously through encoded images* to be given any credence (a therapist's own impressions of the same intervention are similarly vulnerable to considerable distortion and also in need of encoded verification).

As noted, triggers are identified by two means: (1) through *direct recall*, the effort simply to list all known triggers; and (2) by using the clues provided by the narrative themes that have been activated by the trigger and therefore in some disguised fashion portray the trigger event and its implications—the *themes-to-triggers* method.

Mr Drake tried to recall the recent triggers—the frame-related interventions of Ms Brown. She had been holding the frame secured of late, he stated, except for what might have been a slight extension of the previous session—and he was probably wrong about that.

Nothing else came to mind via a direct search of his memory, so he turned to the images in his stories for clues to other triggers—he had already sensed that the uncertain trigger regarding the timing of the end of the last session could not account for the power themes in his stories. The main themes were those of an invasive insect, an attack and being stung (penetrated), the break-in by the robber, and stealing. The only positive theme was the treatment that saved the life of the man who had received multiple bee stings.

In looking at images, once more the first question is: are they frame-securing or frame-modifying? The main frame allusion—the thief forcing open a window—is clearly frame-breaking, and the attack by the bees suggests an assault on interpersonal boundaries. The themes, then, suggest an active frame break, but they are not especially compatible with a possible extension of the duration of the previous session. (In fact, the session had not been lengthened—Mr Drake's watch was wrong). On the other hand, identifying these themes did not modify the conscious-system repression that seemed to be blocking the recall of a strong frame-deviant intervention by Ms Brown. Once more, there was evidence in the encoded themes—the derivative images—that, in contrast to the unknowing conscious system, the deep unconscious wisdom subsystem knew exactly what the missing trigger was.

Mr Drake's next step was to go over all of the themes in this narrative pool and try them out as *bridging themes*—encoded clues as to the nature of the hidden trigger event. Every meaningful narrative pool contains *power themes* (sexuality, the aggression–illness–death group like the robbery, and unrealistic events like the giant bee), which speak for the most compelling unconscious meanings of the active triggers. But there also are *bridging themes*, which represent or portray in encoded fashion the active triggers at the moment—they are *derivatives* of a trigger event.

With the missing trigger still under conscious-system repression, Mr Drake opted strategically to search for the trigger based on the material he had generated to this point in the session, rather than thinking of fresh guided associations to his dream. He began to ferret out and work over the thematic threads of his stories. There were allusions to living room and bedroom, a noise or sound, a huge insect, being stung, a newscast, beehives and multiple stings, medical care, the thief, forcing open a window, theft, money and jewellery, listening to music, and a stereo. Somewhere in this maze of themes there were encoded clues to the missing trigger, clues that had been generated by the deep unconscious system of the mind. Nevertheless, Mr Drake still couldn't find what he was looking for.

For a long while, Ms Brown was also at a loss as to the nature of the specific frame deviation that her patient was working over unconsciously. It is, as I said, quite common for therapists to repress their own frame modifications—unconscious guilt plays a prominent role in this kind of conscious-system repression (the forgetting of a recent and important trigger event).

It was only when Mr Drake went back to his dream for another guided association that her repressive barrier was modified.

The story was about a woman with a morbid fear of bees; she had appeared on a radio talk show with the therapist who had cured her of her fear through deconditioning. Mr Drake had noticed that, ironically, the woman patient had a severe stammer that everyone had ignored in glorifying her newly achieved mental health.

With this encoded narrative, Ms Brown finally modified her defensiveness, and she consciously registered and understood what had been right in front of her all along—the missing trigger was that obvious once the repression was lifted. The pertinent themes initially were somewhat embedded in Mr Drake's stories; they were the allusions to sounds, newscast, and stereo—and finally, the patient and therapist being on a radio talk show.

The key trigger, Ms Brown now realized, must have been a radio interview she had given on the subject of battered wives. The theme of invasiveness supported the likelihood that the broadcast had been heard by Mr Drake. By this means, the therapist had entered her patient's apartment and bedroom (which was where his radio was), breaking into his space in a way that was experienced unconsciously as quite assaultive and dishonest (the thief who broke into his bedroom). It was this frame break that had provoked Mr Drake's own frame break—an eye for an eye, a tooth for a tooth; and a deviation for a deviation. Such is the functional design of the emotion-processing mind.

It took an enormous number of leading queries—a therapist should not identify repressed triggers for his or her patients—before Mr Drake suddenly, and much to his surprise, remembered hearing the interview. He wondered why he had forgotten it, in that (consciously) he had thought Ms Brown was quite impressive and he was glad she was his therapist.

The intensity of Mr Drake's conscious-system repression and defensiveness may appear to be unusual, but, to the contrary, this example is far more the rule than the exception. Also more common than you might expect is the extent to which these defences are shared by both patients and therapists alike. Had Ms Brown not pursued trigger identification and eventually been able to modify her own repressive barriers, it is likely that the trigger would never have surfaced—at least not in this session.

In most forms of standard therapy, there would be fewer encoded images, fewer clues to the repressed trigger, no enhancement of narrative imagery and encoded leads, and no trigger search. There is a strong probability that neither patient nor therapist would ever have recognized the broadcast trigger event and its many ramifications. The therapist's broadcast was a break in the ground rules pertaining to the location of the contact between patient and therapist, the time of that contact, and the relative anonymity of the therapist—it was a very compelling trigger event, indeed.

Notice, too, how easily a standard-model therapist would be able to claim—erroneously but based on his or her field of observation (i.e. the available, but insufficient, manifest material from the patient)—that a broadcast of this kind has little or no effect on patients who happen to hear the show. Even if a patient were to allude to the trigger experience, the conscious appraisal tends to be dismissive or favourable. As a result, without trigger-decoding, a therapist is bound to feel that broadcasts of this kind have positive effects on his or her patients—and therefore do more of them. This is, of course, exactly the opposite of what a trigger-decoding therapist would conclude—or do—based on his or her field of observation (see below).

## PROCESSING THE MISSING TRIGGER

Once the missing trigger was recovered by Mr Drake, he immediately realized that not only must it have been a factor in his frame-deviant referral of the friend to Ms Brown, but it also helped to explain why he had uncharacteristically and for the first time been involved in some petty thievery at work. This latter is, of course, an important behavioural–social consequence of the patient's identification with his frame-breaking therapist.

In the session, once the patient remembered the trigger, the linking of the trigger event to the themes proved relatively easy—some of it was done by the patient, but most of it came from the therapist. While the frame-deviant trigger event had evoked conscious praise and admiration of the therapist by the patient, unconsciously the frame break was experienced as boundary breaking, assaultive, penetrating, toxic, and dishonest.

With this interpretation completed, Ms Brown asked Mr Drake for a fresh association to his dream. Doing so allowed the patient either to validate or to disconfirm the interpretive effort.

> The patient returned again to the story of the man who was stung by the bees. The doctors had done a remarkable job in saving his life. But then, when the police investigated the incident, they discovered that the man had not been wearing clothes beneath his coat and that he had been exposing himself to women in the area. He was arrested, and when he was presented in court to a judge, he swore that the incident with the bees had cured him of his perversion—he'd never expose himself again. The judge did not fully trust his pronouncement and, in sentencing him, included a mandate that the man enter psychotherapy.

This encoded narrative first confirms the therapist's interpretation of the patient's material through a positive image of the doctors' abilities to save the life of the man who had been stung by the bees. This *interpersonally validating image* indicated that through her intervention, Ms Brown was, for the moment, an excellent healer. But the encoded narrative also adds to the interpretation of the material by alluding to the sexual and perverse aspects of Ms Brown's broadcast—her inappropriate exhibition of herself. This addendum provides *cognitive validation* of the therapist's comment through the addition of new material that provides further insight into the unconscious meanings of the trigger event.

Finally, the allusion to the man's pledge never to expose himself again is an excellent model of rectification—the therapist should not do any future broadcasts (i.e. she should secure this aspect of the now-broken frame). Her failure to make this frame-securing pledge is reflected in the story as well, via the allusion to the judge's comment that the man (therapist) could not be entirely trusted and she (the therapist) should get into psychotherapy (to resolve whatever neurotic problems were interfering with the therapist's securing the frame).

## A FURTHER FRAME BREAK

Ms Brown was unable to secure this frame because she had made a commitment to appear on a television interview show on the same topic. The session after she did so, the patient immediately mentioned that he had seen the show. He remarked that Ms Brown looked good on camera and seemed even sharper than when he had heard her on the radio (his conscious-system, denial-based response to this fresh deviation). But then, in turning next to the process of the empowered psychotherapy, he reported that somehow he was unable to remember a dream. He recognized that he therefore had to compose a story so he could have an origination narrative to associate to.

He then made up a story of a being on a tropical island with a beautiful woman and making love to her. His guided associations mainly were about his dreams of meeting a woman he could some day marry and of a professor he once took a course from who was from Tahiti—he was a very wise and thoughtful man.

The trigger for this session was the television appearance by Ms Brown. It is a powerfully frame-deviant and traumatic trigger that flew in the face of previous insights and the acknowledged need to rectify this frame with respect to that kind of exposure by the therapist outside the sessions. In light of the blatancy and repetitiveness of this frame deviation, we might have expected a series of overwhelmingly strong stories with images filled with violence, betrayal, invasiveness, sexual exhibitionism, and disaster. Instead, the images are extremely positive and the allusions are to wise and helpful figures.

We are compelled to postulate that *in the face of this extreme frame-altering trigger event, the deep unconscious system has erected its own (unconscious) repressive and denial barriers for defensive purposes.* The positively toned *encoded* images of wise and helpful figures run counter to the evident hurtful nature of the trigger event. Unconsciously, they support the patient's manifest (conscious) admiration of the therapist and his positive feelings about how she came across in her appearance on television—there is both conscious-system and deep unconscious-system denial.

It appears, then, that when the deep unconscious system experiences an overwhelming trauma, the system invokes deep unconscious repression and denial, and retreats into over-idealizations. Ms Brown would be quite remiss to take these positive images as valid encoded perceptions of her frame break—they are quite out of keeping with its ramifications. Support for this contention is found in the fact that in the following session, one in which this trigger initially was not mentioned, gruesome stories of murderous exhibitionists emerged—along with many other negative images.

Splitting triggers from their encoded themes has already been mentioned as the mind's major communicative defence. In the session in which the trigger was mentioned, there were virtually no derivatives of the patient's unconscious experience. And then, when the incisive harmful encoded perceptions did appear in the patient's material, the trigger event was not mentioned—for the moment it had fallen under the sway of conscious-system repression. Ms Brown was able to work with Mr Drake to elicit the missing trigger and link it to the themes of that session. The work was done in the face of strong resistances, and the patient remained sceptical despite the fit between the trigger and the themes. Encoded validation followed, as did another model of rectification—and this time Ms Brown renounced further public appearances. Additional validating images of genuinely sensitive and helpful figures followed this rectification—and with them, themes of entrapment and annihilation that announced the patient's newly evoked secured-frame anxieties. Such are the cycles of imagery that follow soundly carried-out frame rectifications.

We have explored some fresh clinical material with the architecture of the deep unconscious system of the emotion-processing mind as our main interest. We have also discussed aspects of this system of the mind in a variety of contexts, and the time has come to integrate our understanding of this deep system of the mind into a solid picture of its structure, functions, and world of experience.

CHAPTER NINE

# Essential features of the deep unconscious system

We are now ready to collect our impressions of the deep unconscious system of the emotion-processing mind in order to create a composite picture of this system of the mind. In so doing, it is well to realize that we will be not only characterizing the structural and functional designs of this system, but also developing a picture of *unconscious experience*—the world as seen through unconscious perception (mainly auditory and visual). As we have already observed, this is a very different world from that seen through conscious eyes and ears. It may be difficult to become accustomed to the idea, but we actually live our lives on two distinct plains that share little in common and have only a few connecting links. This suggests, too, that when it comes to psychotherapy, there are two levels on which it is experienced and two very different constellations of techniques and modes of cure, depending on which world a therapist addresses (Langs, 1981, 1985) (see also chapter 10).

## SOME KEY FEATURES

The following appear to characterize best the deep unconscious system of the emotion-processing mind:

1. *The system is an adaptive system with highly effective resources.*

This system is primarily an organ of adaptation, with other functions related to drives, self-scrutiny, and the like assuming secondary roles. In keeping with the alignment of all of the adaptive systems of the human organism, the primary focus of its attention is environmentally directed, with a secondary focus on internal (inner) experience. It is, then, a processing system with its own intelligence, values, needs, self-observing capabilities, memory system, coping resources, sources of anxiety, and so forth.

2. *The system is designed to process automatically emotionally charged inputs that overtax conscious-system resources.*

The deep unconscious system deals with immediate states of conscious-system overload and processes excessively charged and intolerable emotional inputs into the human mind. The architecture of the mind is such that this shift away from conscious registration to unconscious perception is carried out automatically at the perceptual level.

This postulate implies that there must be tracts running from human intellectual-assessing systems to the perceptual apparatus. In neurological terms, it suggests reverse-direction tracts from the cortical and other brain centres to the organs of sensory intake.

3. *The organs of perception that receive inputs from the environment (raw experiences and their meanings) operate outside awareness.*

*Subliminal perception* (auditory, visual, tactile, etc.) is the receptive mode for this system, so that the entire sequence that moves from intake to output occurs without awareness. It seems likely that conscious registration precludes entry into and processing by this deep system; inputs that reach awareness are processed by the conscious system and stored in the superficial unconscious subsystem. In substance, then, the type of registration—conscious or unconscious—determines the processing system that will respond adaptively to an incoming stimulus and its various interrelated but distinctive meanings.

It is well to be clear that there are both design/structural factors and dynamic factors involved in the type of registration that a given stimulus and a particular meaning experiences. For example, powerful implications of frame-deviant triggers, which tend to generate both internal anxiety and disturbing views of the other person (e.g. the therapist as perceived by the patient), tend to be subjected to perceptual repression and shifted to subliminal perception.

4. *The realm of deep unconscious experience of the world is strongly focused on frame impingements.*

It may be difficult to fathom a world of experience that is so concentrated on one group of inputs, but, as I have pointed out, it is a crucial group, to be sure. While our conscious attention roams widely, our deep unconscious attention is sharply focused on settings, ground rules, contexts, and frames. Because it appears that this focus is where much of the action of human emotional life takes place, the deep unconscious system can rightfully be thought of as a highly efficient system.

There are other types of inputs that this system processes (and more may be discovered). The first is the extent to which someone is being helpful or hurtful—for the patient, this refers mainly to the therapist. Attention is also paid to the degree of danger and anxiety connected with communicating about a particular unconscious perception. When a therapist has behaved in an especially traumatic fashion, or a patient has obtained very disturbing information about his or her therapist, the deep unconscious system will tend to invoke denial mechanisms and generate positive encoded images. The system will, however, also encode the deeply experienced danger involved in working over the issue at hand.

This system will also process the *level of meaning* that is being addressed. Thus, patients unconsciously monitor their therapists' preference for manifest-content/implications listening and formulating compared to addressing latent-content/trigger encoded meanings—essentially the level of experience that a therapist deals with.

5. *The system is always focused on and processing the immediate interaction within which it finds itself.*

The deep unconscious system is focused on the here-and-now. In therapy, this means that, unconsciously, a patient continuously monitors the nature and validity of a therapist's silences and active interventions. In addition, once a given session begins, the experience of the immediate frame conditions reactivates all of the therapist's recent frame-related interventions—the deep system processes these impingement over one or more weeks. The narrative material generated in a particular session will therefore reflect via *condensation* the patient's unconscious processing of all triggers that are active at the moment.

Put simply, the deep unconscious system is centred on the recent and immediate frame-related present. The system will anticipate the future or turn to the past only when a contemporaneous trigger arouses and is linked with that future or past (frame-pertinent) event. This includes any announcement of a future frame impingement, as when a therapist indicates his or her plans for a vacation, a fee change, a missed session, etc. The patient also will process his or her own comparable frame-related announcements.

In comparison, while the conscious system also gives primary attention to the present situation in which it is operating, it more freely turns to the past or future, in part as they are related to present circumstances. This reflects the wider range of conscious-system concerns and adaptations as compared to the deep unconscious system.

6. *The adaptive preferences of this system consistently point towards frame-securing options.*

The encoded messages emitted by the deep unconscious system always indicate that frame maintenance and frame-securing are the optimal choices in managing a frame of therapy. In this respect, the system, as I noted, is in opposition to the conscious system's tendency to advocate frame modifications.

7. *The deep unconscious system has its own memory-storage subsystem and its own repressive and denial defences.*

Here too we must become accustomed to an unusual realization: deep unconscious experiences—and they are, in general, highly traumatic and disturbing—can be retrieved from memory *only in encoded narrative form*. There is, then, no direct recall of unconsciously perceived experiences and meanings, and no direct retrieval of the deep system's processing efforts. Deeply repressed events and their meanings unconsciously affect human behaviour and emotional life, but their definition and nature can be fathomed only through narrative thematic communications—they do not emerge whole cloth from deep repression.

There is as well deep unconscious *repression and denial*. The former operates to bar from expression *any encoded version* of a disturbing unconscious experience. In the therapy situation, we hypothesize this form of *repression* when there is a powerful and active frame-related trigger (e.g. the therapist inadvertently forgot a patient's session) and there is an absence of encoded themes of abandonment, betrayal, madness, and such. Deep unconscious *denial* would be evidenced when a traumatic trigger is responded to with positive and idealizing imagery (e.g. the patient speaks of helpful and caring figures in his or her life in a session after the therapist has missed the previous one).

8. *The deep unconscious system has developed its adaptive capacities and intelligence through unconscious experience and unconscious learning.*

From infancy onward, especially once language capacities are in place, the human child unconsciously (subliminally) takes in experiences of all kinds and processes them outside awareness, engaging in deep unconscious learning. It will be essential to study children in order to determine if the focus of the deep unconscious system on rules, frames, and boundaries is genetically wired into the design of the mind, or if this concentration is a learned focus created by deep emotional experiences of the frame impingements a child experiences day in and day out. Some combination of heredity and experiential learning is the likely basis for the design of this deep unconscious system of the mind.

9. *The deep unconscious system embodies ego, id, and superego functions and is especially distinguished by possessing a remarkably incisive adaptational intelligence.*

The deep unconscious system has its own distinctive set of needs (healthy drives and wishes), values and self-functions (strong capacities for self-observation and sound values), and adaptive capacities (especially its deep wisdom). As for deep intelligence, it appears that we learn best in the emotional domain when that learning is taking place outside our awareness.

The system also has remarkably strong and ideal expectations. This is seen in a patient's encoded definition of the ideal frame which includes such delicate needs as not seeing patients on minor legal and religious holidays, expectations of the therapist's presence without interruption at all sessions (every vacation is experienced as a significant abandonment), and the expectation of a truly ideal frame in all respects.

10. *The coping system of the deep unconscious mind is able to process or adapt to multiple inputs simultaneously.*

The system processes multiple meanings simultaneously and generates narrative messages that *condense* the results of the processing of several triggers into a single-storied communication. Thus, the communicative outputs of the system are two-tiered, multiple-meaning productions. In contrast, the conscious system is a linear-processing system that can work over only one trigger and one meaning at a time and respond with one thought or reaction at a time as well. The processing and adaptive capabilities of the deep unconscious system seem far more effective than those of the conscious mind.

11. *The adaptive responses of the deep unconscious system are always encoded and do not break through directly into awareness.*

To discover the presence and nature of unconscious experience and adaptations, trigger-decoding must be employed—there is no other known way to access the workings of this deep system of the mind. *The sole means of expression available to the deep unconscious system is that of disguised (encoded) narrative images.*

12. *The adaptive wisdom of this system finds a communicative outlet in encoded narratives, but it is does not substantially influence direct, conscious coping.*

Because unconscious processing reaches awareness in *encoded* form, its invaluable adaptive preferences are unknown to the conscious mind. Furthermore, these deep levels of understanding and responsiveness do not have substantial unconscious mental connections to the conscious system. As a result, they have virtually no silent or unconscious effect on conscious adaptive choices.

This aspect of the architecture of the mind—which is quite surprising—seems to be a major design flaw in the evolved emotion-processing mind. The trade-off here seems to be that of psychological protection against the terror of becoming aware of horrifying perceptions of others and self *versus* tolerating that awareness (and the guilt, rage, and dread it would evoke) in order to have available far more sound adaptive responses than those forged by the conscious system. A major result of the present design of the mind is conscious-system ineptness in the emotional sphere, combined with deep unconscious effectiveness, which is, however, unavailable as a coping resource. The only way to overcome this structural-functional defect is by trigger-decoding available narrative material in light of evocative triggers. Unfortunately, the conscious system is, by design, not inclined to move in this direction; it takes a significant amount of determination and effort to overcome our natural, design-based resistances to engage in trigger-decoding—a problem that has created many obstacles in our search for deeply effective forms of therapy.

13. *A major consequence of the architecture of the emotion-processing mind is that not only do we employ displacement as a primary mental mechanism, but we also live much of our emotional lives through unconscious and unrecognized displacements that both relieve anxiety and confound our lives.*

The architecture of the mind—reinforced by psychodynamics—is such that the separation of triggers from encoded themes and the obliteration of deep encoded meaning is a prime psychological defence. This splitting of triggers and encoded themes, supplemented by conscious-system repression and denial, is the major protective mechanism that the mind has devised against the anxiety-provoking awareness of traumatic triggers and their most disturbing implications and meanings. Efforts to overcome this alignment of forces and design meet universally with overwhelming obstacles.

In this light, a well-known mental mechanism—*displacement*—assumes an importance in emotional life that has not been fully appreciated. Both human communication and human behaviour are affected by deep unconscious experience. Traumatic triggers are experienced unconsciously and processed adaptively by the deep unconscious wisdom system. Communicatively, these efforts and their adaptation-evoking triggers are not alluded to directly but via displacement, in disguise. Displacement is therefore essential to well-defended emotionally charged communication.

In addition to the communicative use of displacement, the mechanism plays a role in behaviour and symptom formation. The well-advised adaptations of the deep unconscious system are not applied to a trigger event but surface elsewhere. This means that the deep source of an emotional disturbance is not resolved and that the resultant damage and anxiety continues to have its effects.

In addition, the hurtful aspects of unconscious perceptions and experiences, and the fear and guilt that they engender (see below), influence behavioural and emotional responses. But because the trigger event has been repressed, the behavioural consequences are not manifestly directed at the source of the difficulty, but elsewhere via the automatic invocation of displacement. Displacement plays a pivotal role in keeping unconscious experience outside awareness and in facilitating its disguised expression, but its use means that we react to a repressed, traumatic trigger event in the wrong place and with the wrong person(s)—a highly problematic outcome.

In essence, when a therapist intervenes in a traumatic fashion, the patient, in order to keep the trigger and its meanings repressed, will respond to the hurt elsewhere—usually in a relationship outside therapy. The only exceptions to this architecturally designed course of events are seen when the hurt is extreme (e.g. an overt sexual overture, an arbitrary and unjustified increase in the fee, a direct verbal or physical attack of the patient, etc.), in that some, but certainly not all, patients will react directly and challenge or quit the therapist who has done such major harm.

Mr Adams heard his therapist on the radio. But he did not work over and cope with that stimulus directly in any extended fashion—consciously, he found the situation interesting and dismissed it without further thought. But he did work over the frame-related trigger event and adapted to it unconsciously, as revealed by his dream and his guided associations to the dream.

Behaviourally, the hurtful aspects of the trigger did not lead to a criticism of the therapist or a direct threat to terminate the therapy. Instead, these responses were displaced into his job situation, where he stole some money and unjustifiably criticized his boss and threatened to quit his job because the boss had presented some of Mr Adams's work to other people, supposedly without Mr Adams's permission (this was common practice and in no way inappropriate).

Whatever his conscious motives (and they were insubstantial) for these behaviours, they were being driven by powerful unconscious perceptions of his therapist and of the meanings of her frame-deviant actions. Both Mr Adams's behaviours and their most compelling motives had been subjected to repression and displacement. He was responding to a repressed trigger event in the wrong place, and the result was maladaptive.

The extensive use of displacement is inherent to the architecture of the mind. The basic design is for emotionally charged impingements to be adapted to only minimally in the direct situation where the trigger event has taken place. The most critical meanings of the trigger experience are perceived unconsciously and processed by the deep unconscious system, and then reacted to behaviourally somewhere other than the locale of the original evocative event. We work over emotional issues most intensely in situations other than the locale of the trauma—we work them over via displacement.

Behaviourally, our direct reaction to a trigger event tends to be muted. Many traumatic triggers—e.g. obviously erroneous and hurtful interventions by therapists—are accepted without question by patients or reacted to with little or no protest. Instead, the disruptive response to the disturbing trigger event takes place with someone else in some other circumstance. The therapist is hurtful, and the patient hurts someone else or terminates a sound relationship outside therapy, using conscious-system rationalizations to cover over the fact that the *unconscious motives* for the action have unwittingly been displaced from the therapy situation into the personal life of the patient.

Therapists have failed to appreciate the extent to which a patient's symptoms and untoward interpersonal actions are displaced responses to their own errant interventions. The mechanism is invoked both to protect against overwhelming anxiety and rage, and to maintain an over-idealized picture of the therapist. But these defensive displacements by patients foster therapist-denial of the deep link between their interventions (many of them frame-deviant) and their patients' symptomatic behaviours and suffering.

We live much of our emotional lives through displacements, never recognizing the unconscious determinants of our behaviours and symptoms. While patients do occasionally displace onto their therapists reactions that are motivated by events outside treatment, the vast majority of displaced moments run the other way—unconsciously, from the therapist and therapy towards people in the everyday life of the patient. Technically, tracking the vicissitudes of these outside relationships as reflections of the happenings within the therapy is an excellent guide to what is going right and going wrong in the treatment situation.

A sound maxim would have therapists hold themselves and their interventions accountable for all untoward reactions and behaviours of their patients—and much that is positive as well. All of the behaviours and symptoms of a patient should be thought of as trigger-evoked by his or her therapist. We could learn a great deal about sound psychotherapy in this way (see chapter ten).

14. *When subjected to severely traumatic and hurtful triggers, the deep unconscious system will shut down its usually unencumbered processing capabilities in favour of defensive repression, denial, over-idealization, and the invocation of other manic defences.*

As noted above, the deep unconscious system tends to respond initially to severely harmful triggers with a sparseness of derivative images and denial-based positive narratives and themes. As a rule, with time, the system recovers its processing capabilities, and the negative narrative material soon emerges—though often in the absence of a conscious allusion to the hurtful trigger that has evoked them.

15. *Overall, the relative nondefensiveness of the deep unconscious system stands in marked contrast to the enormous defensiveness of the conscious system.*

In principle, in order to ascertain emotionally charged reality and truths, one must be wary of conscious appraisals and thinking and turn instead to their unconscious counterparts as discerned through trigger-decoding. The mind is designed to favour conscious deception and falsifications, and unconscious honesty and truths.

16. *There are two major subsystems of this part of the emotion-processing mind—a deep unconscious wisdom subsystem and a fear/guilt subsystem.*

The fear/guilt subsystem embodies a very influential constellation of *unconscious guilt* and *death-related anxieties*. The guilt accumulates over the years in response to real and fantasied hurts of others and self; it is a powerful unconscious motivating force in human behaviour. Indeed, the plethora of self-defeating behaviours of patients (and therapists) within and outside of psychotherapy attests to the extent to which the fear/guilt subsystem is unconsciously linked to the conscious system and thereby affects overt behaviour and direct adaptation. In addition to psychodynamic factors, then, the human mind is designed to favour self-punishing conscious adaptive decisions—another peculiarity and seeming flaw of the evolved emotion-processing mind.

The second component of the fear/guilt subsystem—that of personal death anxiety—reflects the unconscious embodiment of much of our continuous dread of personal demise. Death anxiety is a strong unconscious motivating force in conscious adaptations; it helps to account for many irrationally defensive behaviours and other forms of psychopathology—especially the over-use of conscious-system denial and manic-like behaviours.

The probable basis for this aspect of the design of the mind lies with the ways in which both unconscious guilt and death anxiety function to restrain our natural inclinations towards externally directed violence towards others. It seems evident, however, that this arrangement has not been especially successful on the individual and social levels. This serves to remind us that the emotion-processing mind probably began to be configured with the development of hominid language about 100,000 to 150,000 years ago—our emotion-processing minds are only at the very beginnings of their evolutionary development.

## SUMMING UP

Deep unconscious experience is initiated by unconsciously perceived events and their unconsciously appreciated meanings. It is centred on the present moment, frame-focused, highly effective in its processing and coping abilities, but capable of only encoded language expression, without much effect on direct adapting efforts. With respect to psychotherapy and our quest for our optimal interventions as therapists, an understanding of this aspect of the architecture of the mind—however much in its infancy—has many critical implications for therapeutic practice. Let us turn now to a discussion of these considerations.

*PART III*

# CONSEQUENCES OF THE ARCHITECTURE OF THE MIND

CHAPTER TEN

# Techniques of therapy and the design of the mind

While it may seem surprising that developing a model of the mind can have a profound influence on the technique of psychotherapy, there is a strong precedence for these effects. Freud's (1900) first model of the mind, which used the criteria of conscious versus unconscious operations to define the systems of the mind, very much affected his ideas about psychoanalytic technique and cure. For example, the goal of therapy was stated as making the unconscious conscious (a goal that we have seen to be more complex than previously thought, in that contents are unconscious in two very different senses of the term, one related to the conscious system and the other to the deep unconscious system). Another goal was to resolve the conflicts between UCS wishes and CS defences and moral condemnations, as was the intention of helping the patient modify the censorship or defences that barred unconscious contents from awareness.

The advent of the structural hypotheses (Freud, 1923) ushered in a new era for psychoanalytic and psychotherapeutic techniques. Treatment was conceptualized in terms of a new aphorism—where id was, ego should be. Therapeutic work with ego dysfunctions, pathological id expressions, dysfunctional object relations, and superego aberrations and its offshoot in self-pathology defines most of today's structurally oriented therapeutic efforts. The issue of conscious versus unconscious mental contents, meanings, conflicts, and communications—and their modification—has faded into the background. There remains only a vague sense that something that is unconscious within the patient is being made conscious. Enhancing the ego and relatedness, improving on a wide range of superego functions and capacities, developing a healthy sense of self, and taming the id are the most common basic goals of treatment at the present time.

All of these efforts are, as we saw, without a foundation in a sophisticated and necessarily complex model of the emotion-processing mind, nor are they grounded in a basic understanding of conscious and unconscious communication. The absence of a sense of basic structure, of a clear means of *unconscious* confirmation for all therapist-interventions, and the view of the mind as a single entity allow for a latitude and even looseness of intervening that cannot help but lead to and sanction ultimately hurtful interventions.

There is another reason to be suspicious of today's practices of psychotherapy, which arises from our fresh understanding of the architecture of the mind. We have seen the extent to which the conscious system of the emotion-processing mind is devoted to defensiveness and self-deception in responding to emotional issues and the degree of influence that deep unconscious fear and guilt have with respect to conscious choices. Psychotherapy has been designed by the conscious minds of psychotherapists without an appreciation for unconscious communication and deep unconscious experience; it has been shaped, too, by an acceptance of the conscious directives and responses of their patients. With the exception of the communicative approach, the wisdom of the deep unconscious system has not participated in the development of psychotherapeutic interventions. As a result, unrecognized but real errors of intervening and unwitting harm are inevitable.

The damage caused by these commonly accepted techniques goes largely undetected because: (1) they are denied and repressed both by patients and by therapists; (2) they satisfy pathological needs in both; (3) their consequences are generally displaced onto figures other than the therapist and are mistakenly accounted for through outside factors rather than therapist-error; (4) they gratify needs in patients to be hurt and punished; and (5) much of the patient's experience of harm is communicated in encoded rather than direct fashion. Since the therapists involved in these situations do not trigger-decode their patients' material, recognition of the deleterious effects of their well-meaning but damaging interventions is all but impossible.

## DESIGN ISSUES IN ASSESSING PSYCHOTHERAPY

Before we define the principles of technique called for by our understanding of the architecture of the mind, let us examine some of the issues clinicians must face if they are to free themselves to make the necessary changes in their ways of working with their patients. The critical issues are these:

1. *The human mind is designed to be unaware of deep unconscious contents and meanings; it is therefore not designed to do psychotherapy in terms of the powerful deep unconscious experiences and the deep unconscious knowledge that have the greatest adaptive power in our emotional lives.*

Until now, the issue of the kind of psychotherapy a therapist chooses to practice has been seen as an intellectual choice with some vague psychodynamic underpinnings. The key issue has been defined as whether or not one decides to pursue the realm of unconscious meaning as in dynamic forms of psychoanalysis and psychotherapy or, instead, opts for a more cognitive approach such as retraining, conditioning, and the like, as in cognitive and gestalt therapies.

However, we can see now that there is a more fundamental factor in this choice, and it involves the essential architecture of the mind. This perspective begins with the realization that evolution and natural selection have created a design of the mind that treats emotionally charged impingements as threats to the survival functions of what appears to be an easily disturbed conscious system—as overloading that system. The design, as we saw, calls for the automatic shunting of heavily charged emotional impingements to unconscious perception and processing in the deep unconscious system of the mind. Furthermore, given that these impingements are threats to the continuing adaptive functioning of the conscious mind, they are confined to deep unconscious memory alone and are barred from entering awareness directly at any time.

Psychotherapy that is truly designed to modify this barrier to consciousness therefore flies in the face of human nature and must overcome or modify the basic architectural configuration of the human psyche. We are compelled to pursue this goal as a *therapeutic necessity* because among the compromises wrought by natural selection, the overuse of repression, denial, and displacement creates many situations in which this protective armamentarium malfunctions or is overly costly and leads to emotional symptoms and interpersonal difficulties. That is, the overly-defensive design of the mind proves to be costly because it causes a degree of suffering in everyone—and a great deal of suffering in many. We also need to work against the architecture of the mind because psychotherapy designed by virtue of conscious-system considerations is inherently harmful to both patients and therapists on some level. To lessen the detrimental consequences of the design of the mind, we have an inviolate responsibility to fathom the deep unconscious experiences we naturally abhor so that we can suitably modify their ill effects.

This discussion implies that any form of psychotherapy that does not use trigger-decoding as its central means of formulating the material from patients—the strong adaptive approach—is not accessing deep unconscious meaning and therefore is not dealing with the most compelling unconscious meanings and processes related to the patient's emotional issues. It also implies that the therapists so involved cannot appreciate the unconsciously transmitted ramifications of their interventions—be they helpful or hurtful.

Today's psychodynamically oriented psychotherapists are dealing with the implications of manifest material and thinly disguised images that are part of the domain of experience and adaptation dealt with by the conscious system. Other, more cognitive, forms of therapy work with the direct adaptations and communications of the conscious system and do not touch on communications from either the superficial unconscious subsystem or any aspect of deep unconscious experience. To state it again, the basic configuration of the mind pushes therapists in these directions.

To summarize this point, the first obstacle to sound, adaptively informed psychotherapy is to be found in the basic architecture of the mind as it precludes access to deep unconscious contents and even creates defences against the expression and understanding of encoded or derivative expression of such contents. We may think of this as *the natural dread of unconscious meaning and experience*—a design influence that must be overcome if more effective therapeutic work is to be done (Langs, 1984–85).

2. *The human mind is also designed to favour deviant rather than secured frames consciously, in that the deepest and most intense anxieties that humans experience are secured-frame anxieties.*

Secured-frame anxieties are closely linked with death anxiety—the claustrum qualities of the secured frame are experienced deeply as the claustrum of life as it is surrounded and encased by death. The human mind has evolved only one basic mechanism to cope with and handle death anxiety—the use of *denial in its myriad of forms*. One form of denial involves *modifying frames* in order to deny one's entrapment in a life that ends with death. This means that by design, the minds of both patients and therapists are unable to cope with death and death-related anxieties through insight; they therefore opt for maladaptive, action-oriented, frame-deviant solutions and forms of treatment that in the long run are very costly and harmful.

The human mind has evolved with psychodynamically driven warning signals—fear and anxiety—that are activated in response to physical and psychological dangers. The mind is less well configured to signal *frame-related dangers*. At times, the dangerous aspects of deviant frames will evoke anxious reactions in those exposed to their consequences. But more often, despite their deeply harmful effects, deviant-frame dangers do not evoke adaptation-mobilizing warning signals.

In similar fashion, we are lacking in a secured-frame danger-signal mechanism despite the morbid fears and dysfunctional behaviours evoked by these health-giving, yet dreaded frames. While patients (and therapists) do respond behaviourally with aversive reactions to secured frames, even as they benefit from their positive qualities, they have no signal that warns them that, unconsciously, they are feeling overwhelmingly threatened by that frame. Many behaviours primarily motivated by wishes to flee secured frames—both within and outside therapy—are rationalized with other reasons (e.g. divorces, extramarital affairs, the selection of blatantly frame-deviant modes of therapy, flight from secured-frame treatment situations). The unconscious secured-frame entrapment and death anxieties that motivate these actions do not create a consciously experienced danger signal—the behaviours lack an affect that would indicate the deep distress that underlies them.

*Unconscious and unfelt secured-frame anxieties* represent the second fundamental reason that psychotherapists are averse to working with the deep unconscious system of the mind (Langs, 1984–85). This system, as you will recall, consistently advocates and validates secured-frame interventions and invalidates frame-deviant efforts. Indeed, deep unconscious meaning and secured frames are two sides of the same coin—embracing one goes with embracing the other, much as avoiding one goes with avoiding the other. Given their own unresolved secured-frame anxieties, therapists are loath to work within secured frames or to trigger-decode their patients' frame-evoked narratives lest they be faced with powerful encoded directives to establish or maintain secured frames. Again, we must remember that *we pay a significant price* for these avoidances in the harm they cause to ourselves as therapists and to our patients—there is something inherently destructive in every frame modification.

The deep unconscious system of the psychotherapist continuously monitors his or her therapeutic work. While a therapist may well be consciously satisfied with his or her efforts according to conscious-system criteria (which are, of course, quite unreliable and often misguided), deep unconscious satisfaction comes only from validated trigger-decoded interpretations and secured-frame management responses. Failing these unconsciously defined criteria of truly helpful interventions, the nonvalidated therapist will unconsciously perceive the harm done to his or her patient and experience unconscious guilt. Unwittingly and unconsciously, he or she will then seek out a wide range of self-punishments—in both the professional and the personal realms. *Deep unconscious guilt is the major disease of today's psychotherapists*, who are paying an enormous price for their well-meaning but often harmful ways.

In this light, sound and unconsciously validated psychotherapy may be thought of as an attempt to overcome the costly flaws in the evolved architecture of the mind, carried out by a psychotherapist motivated to overcome those flaws. Such a therapist is somehow prepared to enter with his or her patient the world of deep unconscious experience in all its awesome splendour and deep dread. It is here that all concerned will discover the most powerful unconscious forces in a patient's emotional dysfunctions and alleviate symptom complexes through sound and validated trigger-decoded interpretations and the healing aspects of secured and securing frames.

## THE TECHNIQUE OF PSYCHOTHERAPY AND THE DESIGN OF THE MIND

What, then, are some of the directions that the technique of psychotherapy is likely to take once our understanding of the design of the mind takes hold? The following appear to be most notable:

1. *There will be a change in how therapists listen to and formulate the material from their patients.*

Current practice makes use of manifest contents and their conscious and unconscious implications, to which are added purported genetic links. The new approach will use trigger-decoding as the primary means of deciphering unconscious meaning and will append genetic connections to that centre point as they emerge in the material from patients. Formulations will move away from a concentration on the mind of the patient either in isolation or as it responds through fantasy to the interaction with the therapist—the intrapsychically centred paradigm. In its place, there will be a largely interactional-adaptational focus in which the mind of the patient is seen as adapting to the specific interventions of the therapist—first and foremost, in terms of unconscious perception (rather than fantasy), with secondary reactions to these perceptions in the form of adaptive suggestions, models of rectification, genetic stirrings, fantasy formations, and the like.

2. *The ground rules and setting—the framework of therapy, its management by the therapist and impingements by the patient—will move from a peripheral position in the thinking of psychotherapists to the centre of their perspectives on the treatment experience.*

As we have seen, conscious-system psychotherapists relegate the frame to the background of the therapeutic interaction and technically adopt a loose if not cavalier attitude towards frame impingements. Frame-related interventions by therapists and frame-related behaviours by patients are seldom noticed and almost never appreciated for their profound importance. While certain blatant frame breaks, like sexual contact between a patient and therapist, are now looked upon as unmistakably deviant and harmful, the breadth and depth of the unconscious effects of lesser frame lapses are barely understood. Beyond the more outrageous frame alterations, manifest-content listening is unable to generate a consensus as to the ideal frame and the impact of frame modifications.

The new forms of psychotherapy will fully recognize the central role played by ground-rule impingements for the deep unconscious experience and emotional lives of both patients and therapists. Psychotherapy will become frame-centred and will stress the need to offer patients as secured a frame as possible. Rectification of frame deviations at the behest of the patient's derivative or encoded narratives and the trigger-decoded interpretation of all frame-related transactions will be among the most frequent interventions made by therapists.

This kind of work will be recognized as the essence of cure. Such work provides patients (and therapists) with an optimal healing setting and background experience. It allows for the insightful working-through of foreground frame issues as they become activated by actions of either party to therapy. It also enables the therapist to connect the patient's unconscious experience to the patient's life history and psychopathology. The secured frame is also the best setting for the resolution of pathological forms of death anxiety. All in all, these efforts will provide patients with the most profound and useful insights available today, while affording them an ideal opportunity for unconscious introjective identifications with a healthy and truly effective therapist who is capable of securing and sustaining the secured frame and correctly interpreting frame-related issues and conflicts.

3. *There will be a far better understanding of the nature of conscious-system forms of psychotherapy in ways that can enhance the effectiveness of these modes of treatment.*

As therapists, we are committed to understanding deeply the nature and effects of our formulations and interventions. As such, we must in time use our understanding of the architecture of the mind to illuminate standard forms of therapy. There are many patients and therapists who are unable to tolerate the deep meanings and insights, and the experience of a secured frame, that are a vital part of trigger-decoding forms of psychotherapy. We are therefore obligated to search for the best forms of treatment that these patients can tolerate and benefit from.

At present, treatment modes such as these are dominated by conscious-system thinking. The shift to deep unconscious system thinking will clarify the many false beliefs therapists have developed regarding these forms of treatment and help to identify their damaging aspects. In all, turning to deep unconscious wisdom will facilitate the establishment of more effective versions of these surface-oriented forms of therapy.

Although it seems likely that every patient is entitled to a try at adaptation-oriented forms of therapy—it is at the moment the optimal mode of symptom alleviation and the form of treatment with the highest *help/hurt ratio*—we must be better prepared to treat patients who are unable to do so. Most of these patients suffer from early or recent highly traumatic near-death or death-related experiences and are unable to tolerate any expression of the unconscious meanings of these events. The unconscious guilt and rage that these incidents evoke seem so overwhelming to these patients that they cannot tolerate interactional–adaptive forms of therapy.

Conscious-system symptom alleviation is always costly, but the price can be minimized by attempting to modify extreme defences and to enhance a patient's least pathological defences as well. These modes of therapy can support and strengthen conscious-system defences like repression and denial, but clearly there is the risk of overdoing these defences to the point where they are distinctly self-defeating for the patient.

Other means of relief are inherently more damaging. Conscious-system therapists may bring momentary relief to their patients through such means as sanctioning pathological behaviours, thereby lessening the patient's *conscious* guilt. These therapists also may promote the excessive and costly overuse of denial and repression, or support action-discharge behaviours that ultimately are harmful to the patient and others. There may also be an unconscious source of relief for a patient in that the therapist behaves in a more dysfunctional fashion than does the patient—cures through unconscious perceived nefarious comparison (Langs, 1985).

The frame deviations invoked by these therapists may also bring temporary relief to the patient—again at great cost to all concerned. And, finally, relief may be gained through the obliteration of deep unconscious meaning, a form of denial that is supported by the offer of false formulations designed to allow for a pretence at insight when either none has evolved or the insight is functionally useless or of only minimal value.

The face of psychotherapy could change radically through a full appreciation for the architecture of the mind. It is an area of psychoanalytic understanding that needs a great deal of clinical and formal research. For now, we should take what we have learned about the architecture of the mind, make full use of it, and not succumb to conscious-system defences that are undermining the entire field of psychotherapy.

*CHAPTER ELEVEN*

# Syndromes of dysfunctional design

Historically, each of the major shifts in psychoanalytic thinking not only led to new ways of viewing the world of emotional difficulties and their cure, but also brought with it realizations of new forms of emotional dysfunction—previously unrecognized clinical syndromes. Theory does indeed give fresh eyes for observing, and new ways of looking at the therapeutic interaction inevitably generate fresh perspectives on all aspects of the psychotherapeutic endeavour.

The topographic theory (Freud, 1900) of UCS, PCS, and CS stressed the intrapsychic conflicts that arise between the systems UCS and CS, and the repression of incestuous and aggressive wishes. Psychopathological syndromes were largely defined in terms of inner conflict and the excessive use of repression and censorship. The advent of the structural hypotheses (Freud, 1923) brought with it the recognition of a host of new syndromes—ego dysfunctions; disorders of self-image, self-esteem, and self-regulation; interpersonal disorders and the like.

The introduction of the strong adaptive viewpoint and knowledge of the architecture of the emotion-processing mind have also brought with them the realization of a new set of emotional dysfunctions. These disorders have their basis in the means by which the emotion-processing mind deals with emotionally charged inputs. *Essentially, they reflect dysfunctions in the processing of emotionally charged information and meaning.*

Clinically, the syndromes that stem in large measure from these maladaptive changes in the emotion-processing mind are both familiar and unfamiliar. They take the form of commonplace problems like repetitively making poor and self-hurtful choices in work, love, and other relationships, failing to achieve life goals, and a wide range of well-recognized symptom complexes and interpersonal and characterological disorders. But they also manifest themselves as more subtle disturbances in work, relating, and living one's life—generally unnoticed maladaptations that nonetheless reflect impairments in the processing capacities of the emotion-processing mind.

Heretofore, there has been no means of recognizing that there is a deep source of this myriad of emotional difficulties in a dysfunction of the emotion-processing mind. Indeed, all symptom complexes and interpersonal difficulties reflect, at the deepest level, some type of processing disturbance. We are, then, dealing with a fundamental psychological problem that cannot be resolved in standard forms of therapy, where it is not recognized. But even when the syndrome has been identified through adaptational–communicative listening and formulating, it proves difficult to ameliorate. Indeed, at times the processing dysfunction reflects a lasting reconfiguration of the architecture of the mind.

## SYSTEM OVERLOAD

In principle, every system has a threshold for its processing capacities, beyond which it goes into *system overload* and malfunctions (Langs, 1992c). This constraint inevitably applies to the emotion-processing mind and each of its two main systems—conscious and deep unconscious. The manifestations of these system failures are not seen in gross breakdowns of mental functioning as in the psychoses, but in far more subtle forms of conscious and unconscious failures in adequately representing and processing the meanings and experience of emotionally charged triggers—and the resultant failures of adaptation.

As noted, these difficulties can be identified only through an interactional–adaptive approach to listening and formulating, and a study of the means by which the two systems of the mind process activating trigger events. This effort calls for the identification of frame-related triggers; an evaluation of conscious responses to the trigger; an assessment of the imagery—if any—that is evoked by those triggers; an evaluation of the success of the linking process that connects triggers to encoded themes to reveal unconscious meaning and experience; and a full appreciation of the vicissitudes of a patient's self-indicators—mainly, the course of his or her symptom complexes and resistances to therapy.

Using these tools, we are in a position to draw conclusions as to how the mind is coping with its adaptation-evoking triggers and infer the prevailing design and functioning of the emotion-processing mind. To do so, we need a proper framework—we must supplement standard psychodynamic theory with a viable systems theory and a definition of the architecture of the emotion-processing mind. The former has been offered in detail in an earlier book (Langs, 1992c) and is presented briefly below, while the latter is, of course, the subject of the present volume. With these perspectives in hand, we will be prepared to observe the mind in action and discuss its capacities, limitations, and dysfunctions.

## *TYPES OF PROCESSING DISORDERS*

There are two broad and interrelated classes of processing system dysfunctions—*short-term malfunctions and long-term reconfigurations of the emotion-processing mind.* Furthermore, the processing impairment may affect either the conscious system or the deep unconscious system—or both, as is most often the case.

*Conscious-system* malfunctions are reflected in disruptions to cognitive and direct coping skills which generally stem from the over-use of obliterating defences like denial and repression. The symptomatic consequences may be encapsulated and neurotic, or pervasive and a sign of psychosis. On the other hand, deep unconscious system dysfunctions are reflected in failures to generate meaningful and interpretable communicative networks in response to traumatic trigger events. These dysfunctions may also be pervasive or restricted to a particular class of overly sensitive triggers.

*Short-term processing malfunctions* generally arise when there is an immediate, traumatic input (trigger) that overtaxes the processing capacities of the emotion-processing systems so that the input is not properly worked over and metabolized, and some degree of emotional disorder transpires. In the more enduring situation, there is a redesigning of the emotion-processing mind, with major consequences for how information and meaning are handled and adapted to. This redesign greatly increases a patient's resistances to achieving deep insight and aggravates his or her symptomatic picture—and the overall quality of his or her life.

In both types of dysfunction, the extent of the disruption in the architecture of the mind and its adaptive capabilities depends mainly on two factors: first, on the nature, power, and demand for processing and adapting that a given stimulus or trigger event places on the mental systems; and, second, on the state and capabilities of the system at the time of the disruptive input.

These processing dysfunctions are quite real and are in evidence in far more individuals—patients and therapists—than one might think. Unfamiliarity with these syndromes is entirely due to the failure of dynamic therapists to engage in trigger-decoding. Indeed, the amelioration of each of these syndromes—the restoration of an optimal configuration to the architecture of the mind—poses an unrecognized major challenge for today's psychotherapists.

## SHORT-TERM SYSTEM OVERLOAD

The syndrome of *short-term system overload*, as it occurs in psychotherapy, may develop in either the patient or the therapist—and, not infrequently, in both simultaneously (e.g. when a frame-deviant trigger event overtaxes the processing systems of both). The syndrome is usually set off by a strongly charged frame-related trigger event—and it may be either frame-deviant or frame-securing. More rarely, the syndrome may occur when a party to therapy is heavily burdened with the ongoing processing of existing emotionally charged triggers and a moderately strong trigger event evokes system shutdown or dysfunction. This type of situation typically occurs when there have been chaotic transactions related to the ground rules of a therapy—e.g. repeated frame modifications or many shifts back and forth from frame-securing to frame-modifying. The energy requirements needed to deal mentally with these disturbing events place too great a demand on the mind's processing capacities—especially those of the deep unconscious system—and a breakdown in processing occurs.

In this regard, we may note that we have already seen that the conscious system is protected by design from system overload through the automatic shunting of painful perceptions and meanings to subliminal perception and unconscious processing. Nevertheless, the system may still be overwhelmed when a trauma is acute and blatantly destructive—e.g. an act of physical violence by or directed against the patient, the suicide of a loved one or friend, an outrageous assault or seduction of a patient by a therapist, and so forth.

The conscious-system shutdown caused by these triggers is supplemented with a shutdown by the deep unconscious system as well—there are few or no encoded themes to work over and/or poor or no representations of the trigger event to link to the themes that are available. These kinds of triggers may also create processing-system dysfunctions that become long-term as well (see below).

## SOURCES OF DYSFUNCTION

In citing examples of triggers that tend to evoke this kind of short-term processing dysfunction, let us turn first to patients. They may suffer this type of design failure when a therapist modifies the frame by revealing personal information about his or her social life, or when a third party to therapy does so and passes on especially traumatic information to the patient—e.g. a serious illness afflicting the therapist or a member of his or her family, a dishonest act such as professional malpractice, information about another patient whom the therapist is seeing, or any other personal information that is grossly disturbing. Patients may also suffer processing breakdowns after repetitive lesser frame modifications and, at times, when the frame is secured, arousing death and other anxieties.

It is to be stressed that therapists who are party to these frame deviations and frame-securing moments often suffer from processing difficulties themselves. While the syndrome is more easily identified in patients (they fail to produce the necessary encoded imagery or prove unable to recover a significant trigger event and therefore fail to process its meanings and impact), the manifestations of processing failures in therapists are more difficult to recognize. The main signs of this problem tend to involve distinct failures in listening, formulating, and intervening.

For example, a therapist may have difficulty remembering a problematic trigger event or, if he or she does so, a blunder is made when trying to connect the trigger to the encoded themes from the patient. Repetitive failures in interpreting and in securing the frame characterize such therapeutic work, but additional emotional dysfunctions may ensue—problems in working with patients in general, other kinds of professional difficulties, and symptomatic disturbances that appear in the therapist's social life.

For both patients and therapists, processing dysfunctions can also arise from overwhelming events external to the therapy relationship. In principle, these dysfunctions cannot be thought of as interactionally produced within the treatment setting. There are, however, three caveats in these cases:

(1) the therapist must remain alert for contributing triggers from within the treatment; (2) the dysfunction may have developed because the emotion-processing mind has been overloaded with the processing of traumatic triggers from within the therapy; and (3) a dysfunction with its primary origins related to triggers outside therapy may nonetheless create processing difficulties that extend to other trigger events, including those within the therapy interaction.

To cite some examples, this syndrome may arise if either party to treatment suffers the death of a family member, friend, or loved one; experiences a sudden injury, illness, or life-threatening trauma; or is directly involved in any type of death-related situation—e.g. the accidental death of a passenger in a car that a patient or therapist was driving, a miscarriage or planned abortion, and such. These traumas usually cause short-term processing dysfunctions, but, again, the functional difficulties may extend into the long term as well.

## PROBLEMS IN TRACING THE EFFECTS OF ERRANT INTERVENTIONS

The problem of tracing the effects of therapists' interventions (triggers) on patients, and the related difficulties in recognizing the clinical consequences of alterations in how patients process emotionally charged information and meaning, are, I believe, among the most important unsolved issues in all of psychotherapy.

The first question lies with asking how we can identify, with relative clinical certainty, the actual and specific effects of a therapist's verbal and behavioural interventions, and his or her management of the ground rules of therapy. This proves to be an exceedingly difficult question to answer because most of these effects are mediated through unconscious processes and revealed via encoded narratives. The consequent emotional dysfunctions tend to be minimized or go unnoticed, or they are dismissed as having causes other than the interventions of a therapist.

Displacement, in particular, plays havoc with efforts to trace the detrimental effects of aberrant therapist-interventions on patients in therapy. Most symptomatic and dysfunctional responses in patients to hurtful inputs from their therapists occur outside of therapy and are seldom linked to their sources within the therapy—mistakenly, they are traced to other events and causes. It seems quite clear that both patients and therapists are, in general, strongly motivated to deny the detrimental consequences of a therapist's efforts. Therapists in this situation need to maintain their positive self-images and belief in their power, expertise, wisdom, and immortality, while patients need to over-idealize their therapists, whom they treat as if they were shamans, priests, and idols, and consciously accept these deeply errant efforts because of unconscious needs for harm and punishment.

In all, then, there are two main factors in the difficulty we encounter in trying to demonstrate convincingly the harmful effects of erroneous interventions and frame deviations by a psychotherapist—the mediation of these effects silently and unconsciously into displaced domains, and the needs in all concerned to deny such happenings.

## AMELIORATIVE MEASURES

How can we counteract these seemingly overwhelming obstacles? The following seem pertinent:

1. We should seek *encoded validation* for every intervention made by a therapist—verbally or with respect to frame management. We also must assume that, in general, a valid intervention is salutary for, and a nonvalidated intervention is inherently harmful to, the patient.
2. We should be on the alert for the emergence of untoward events and harm, from others or self-inflicted, in the life of a patient and in his or her therapy. Usually, such events can and should be traced back to their origins in therapist-made errors. We should assume, too, that every emotional

disturbance, hurtful choice, and dysfunction suffered by a patient (and therapist) stems from at least one significant trigger in the form of an errant intervention. Monitoring symptoms in this way will compel us as therapists to re-examine the effects of our interventions and promote the recognition of well-meaning but hurtful efforts.

3. We should trace the effects of unconsciously validated interventions and confirm their constructive and symptom-alleviating influence on patients—and on their therapists. Clinical experience has already shown this to be the case, but this crucial observation must be confirmed by every psychotherapist who finally invokes trigger-decoding as his or her guide to therapeutic technique.

4. Finally, we need to investigate the problem of identifying *processing dysfunctions* using clinical and formal research methods. For these purposes, we need to supplement clinical observation with the development of *psychological tests* that will tap into the processing activities of the emotion-processing mind and its two distinctive systems. These endeavours need to be directed towards both developmental studies and the investigation of adult processing as it is affected by experiences within and outside therapy.

## MANIFESTATIONS OF SHORT-TERM PROCESSING DYSFUNCTIONS

How, then, can you recognize a short-term aberration in the mental processing of emotionally charged information and meaning?

The following steps will guide you towards the discovery of these dysfunctions in your patients:

1. Identify all active triggers, especially those that are unusual or notably stressful.
2. Observe whether the patient alludes directly to the trigger or does so in clear encoded form (e.g. represents the news of a therapist's being charged with malpractice with a story of a surgeon whose ethics were under attack).

3. Observe whether derivative themes appear in the narrative material, the extent to which there are *both bridging and power themes*, and the ease with which the themes can be linked to the traumatic trigger to yield surprising and compelling decoded (unconscious) meaning and insight.

4. Assess the ease with which the patient carries out the decoding process to the point of linking themes to triggers and arriving at his or her own trigger-decoded interpretation.

5. If interpreting is necessary on your part, note how readily the patient's material facilitates intervening and how well the effort is received by the patient—both consciously and unconsciously. To ascertain the latter response, you must seek encoded validation through subsequent narrative material and observe the extent of confirmation—and how the patient then deals with these added validating images if they materialize. (Keep in mind, too, that nonvalidation calls for reformulation.)

6. Notice whether there are active self-indicators in the form of symptoms or resistances that are connected to the traumatic trigger. These are the emotional difficulties that the processing failure is causing.

These efforts are carried out most easily in empowered psychotherapy, where they are a defined part of the therapeutic work. They are feasible, with some difficulty, in communicative psychotherapy, but they are not feasible in standard forms of therapy in which trigger-decoding is not utilized and processing dysfunctions thereby go unrecognized.

*Indications of processing dysfunction* in patients include the absence of direct or clearly encoded allusions to a strong trigger event, a paucity of encoded narrative material, difficulties in linking, and strong conscious resistances when the therapist attempts to link the trigger to the themes—and to both interpret the material and rectify any modification in the frame that can be corrected. (Encoded validation and positive conscious responses will not materialize if a possible frame rectification is missed.)

Conscious resistances in the presence of encoded validation of a therapist's intervention suggest conscious-system processing dysfunctions. Patients suffering from this disorder will invoke a wide variety of spurious objections to the sound and unconsciously confirmed work of their therapists. On the other hand, *unconscious confirmation* followed by a breakdown in unconscious processing indicates the presence of deep unconscious resistances and processing disturbances. Nevertheless, initial encoded validation of interventions remains a critical safeguard against a therapist's erroneous formulation of the patient's material. Such errors are, of course, generally a result of a therapist's own processing failures.

In substance, then, patients who, over the course of one or two sessions following a strong trigger event, do not generate interpretable communicative networks are manifesting a *short-term processing dysfunction syndrome*. The primary deficit lies within the deep unconscious system, which has all but shut down its adaptive activities and which then generally receives conscious-system support through denial and other resistance mechanisms. The processing disturbance may be confined to a specific, excessively charged trigger or may spread to mental processing and coping in general. As a rule, the deep unconscious system recovers within a week or two and turns to processing and adapting to the overwhelming trigger event—especially if a necessary frame rectification has been invoked.

During the period of difficulty, there is a failure to adapt effectively to the traumatic trigger; insight also cannot be achieved. Relief from the underlying anxiety and depression is not possible on a constructive basis, and the patient is likely to suffer from a variety of emotional dysfunctions.

Of note in this regard are situations in which a powerful frame deviation by a therapist is the active trigger event. Patients typically displace their behavioural reactions from the therapist onto other people in their everyday lives and act out against them, often through social-context frame deviations—all the while covering over the deep unconscious source and motivation for the behaviour with conscious-system rationalizations. Many social-setting frame breaks occur on this basis, and many satisfying relationships have been destroyed in this way.

As noted, this syndrome may, of course, develop in therapists and cause problems in carrying out trigger-decoding. The consequences may also spill over into additional countertransference-based errors in intervening, forms of acting out within and outside therapy, social-setting frame deviations, and other difficulties in their emotional lives. When a therapist experiences a significant emotional event (trigger), he or she should be on the alert for these unconsciously driven, seemingly subtle effects—they have considerable unconscious motivational power. Indeed, issues of this kind undoubtedly underlie therapists' choices of therapeutic approach, moving them either towards or away from deep unconscious meaning and secured or deviant frames. Flight from unconscious meaning and secured frames usually reflects some degree of processing dysfunction.

## DYSFUNCTIONAL MODIFICATIONS IN THE ARCHITECTURE OF THE MIND

The processing overload caused by the stresses of severe traumas may cause significant changes in the architecture of the emotion-processing mind, leading to long-term processing dysfunctions. These disorders may, of course, be experienced by either patients or therapists. While there may be many root causes of these reconfigurations, two kinds of trauma loom large—repeated early life experiences related to death, violence, and inappropriate seduction, and, in adult life, involvement in recent death-related incidents. In addition to these outside sources of restructuring, repeated traumas by a psychotherapist—usually in the form of frame deviations—can create this syndrome in a patient even as he or she rationalizes away the evoked disturbance and continues to work with the damaging therapist. Indeed, with most patients, it takes a major and overwhelmingly destructive action by a therapist to mobilize the conscious system to react—and then, with only certain patients, with direct objections and/or termination of the therapy if the situation is not corrected (if it can be).

The *long-term processing dysfunction syndrome* involves a reconfiguration of the architecture of the mind so that the processing of emotionally charged triggers is maladaptively modified in some lasting manner. Spontaneous recovery from this syndrome is rare—it is far easier to damage the mind than it is to repair it. Even with sound psychotherapy—if the dysfunctional patient will tolerate it (and often they will not)—these overly-defensive alterations in the design of the mind are very difficult to correct.

Communicatively, this syndrome is recognized by the repeated failure of a patient to work over adaptation-evoking emotionally charged triggers successfully. Here, too, the system failure may be restricted to one class of triggers or may generalize to all processing efforts. In addition, the patient will show signs of acute, and especially chronic, emotional difficulties that are difficult to pin down and resolve. These chronic problems are rationalized in terms of outside triggers and the difficulties of daily life and living—their source in the patient's inability to metabolize the effects of traumatic trigger events is entirely unappreciated. These patients always get the bad breaks, make unexpected mistakes and wrong choices, and otherwise suffer despite extensive therapeutic efforts to modify these problems insightfully.

The keys to this syndrome are a relative shutdown in deep unconscious system processing and the use of conscious-system denial and obliteration. The *denial defence* is layered and extends from the conscious system into the deep unconscious system. The patient *denies* that he or she has a problem, that the emotionally charged trigger has any notable meaning, that the encoded themes have any connection to anything, that linking the themes to a trigger event has any relevance to anything important, that the main trigger is not the one at issue—conscious-system negations are almost endless. In addition, in the face of strong and clear derivatives, the patient will deny any connection to an activated trigger. All in all, the resistances to therapeutic work are very strong and may at times lead a patient to find unfounded excuses for terminating his or her therapy prematurely—the flight from deep unconscious meaning and secured frames is intense.

On the encoded level, the narrative images from these patients contain repetitive themes that allude to the dangers of knowing, seeing, probing, going deeper, and understanding (the fear of unconscious meaning) and of entrapment and annihilation (the fear of the secured frame). These deep anxieties—and they always involve an expectation of annihilation—are represented in the patient's material, but the more basic frame issues and their unconscious ramifications, the activating trigger events, are not portrayed and worked over. Connections to the traumas that led to the processing dysfunction are virtually non-existent.

Children who have suffered repetitive childhood traumas of seduction and/or physical and severe psychological harm appear to configure minds that can carry out only minimal amounts of mental processing. Their emotion-processing systems tend to bypass mental coping and metabolizing in favour of discharge through maladaptive actions that tend to be quite harmful in nature.

Similarly, patients who suffer traumatic death-related experiences or have in some way caused a loss of life tend automatically to reconfigure their emotion-processing systems in lasting ways. In an overwhelming effort to obliterate the horrifying unconscious meanings and ramifications of these powerful trigger events, their deep processing capabilities all but shut down and conscious-system denial mechanisms are central to their impaired processing of later trigger experiences. They are left vulnerable to acting out and symptomatic behaviours that reflect their failures in mental coping and adaptation; subtle and chronic maladaptations are commonplace.

These patients are especially unable to process a trigger event that is closely linked to the disruptive trauma. A frame-deviant trigger that would activate the death-related experience will go unprocessed and be subjected to strong conscious-system denial. Even as these patients suffer, they deny the connection to their triggers and remain quite unaware that they are victims of a processing malfunction. Despite their distress, they are also remarkably *unmotivated* to pursue trigger-decoding and deep insight. All a therapist can do is work very slowly and carefully with these patients, moving them towards some degree of deep processing and doing so in doses that they can tolerate—a difficult task at best.

The imagery that occasionally does emerge from these patients indicates that they deeply dread the sense of uncontrolled violence, unconscious guilt, and awareness of personal death and other horrors that would first be expressed in derivative form and then, with trigger-decoding, given access to awareness. These patients are damned if they do not process and adapt to their disturbing triggers, in that they suffer without relief, but they feel that they will be damned if they do process deep unconscious meanings and enter secured frames. In like fashion, their therapists are damned if they work towards unconscious meaning, because the patent will attack them or flee in terror, and damned if they avoid such meaning in that the patient will experience them as more terrified of unconscious meaning than they are, and suffer pathological introjections of the ineffective and frightened therapist.

## *A PERSONAL FRAME-RELATED BLIND SPOT*

I can think of no better way to end this book than with a personal vignette that illustrates the power of conscious-system defences and how they may detrimentally affect the way in which one does psychotherapy—and its supervision. I am, of course, a therapist deeply committed to trigger-decoding and the strong adaptive approach. I have worked the frame, so to speak, for many years now, always learning new things from the deep unconscious system regarding their effects and power. And I have spent much of my career as a therapist securing unrecognized blatant and subtle breaks in the frame as they materialized in my clinical work and supervisory practice—and called for tightening up.

Recently, I wrote a book on the supervisory process and experience (Langs, 1994) that could have been subtitled: "A Reconsideration of Supervision in Light of Its Ground Rules and Frame." In the course of writing the book, I proposed that, in principle, a supervisee should present his or her therapy sessions using process-note material written after the session—and then immediately destroy them. The main rationale for this proposal was that supervisees who present material spontaneously tend to omit critical parts of the sessions and/or consciously or unconsciously revise their presentation in response to the interventions of their supervisors. In presenting a new paradigm that combined empowered psychotherapy with supervision, I maintained the same position on this issue.

Recently, I gave a lecture on the supervisory process. In the course of the discussion, a member of the audience pointed out that I advocate and argue persuasively for nonrecording of any kind by patient or therapist in any form of psychotherapy, yet here I was sanctioning its use in supervision and especially in empowered supervision, where supposedly no records whatsoever are made or kept.

I began to respond with the above-noted rationalizations for this proposal, when I stopped short. I suddenly realized that my discussant was entirely correct: there was no substantial or valid rationale for having supervisees record and present written process-note case material under any circumstances. This requisite violated the basic ground rules of the kind of psychotherapy I was teaching supervisees to value and carry out.

Contradictions of this sort are psychotogenic and unconsciously undermine the teaching effort. They unconsciously generate a picture of a confused supervisor who simultaneously advocates both frame-securing and frame-modifying—and with respect to the same ground rule of the nonrecording of sessions. The frame-altering side of the proposal inevitably would encourage frame breaks by supervisees. The recording of sessions violates the ground rules of total privacy and total confidentiality beyond the absolute minimum needed in supervision—which is the only way a student can learn how to do effective psychotherapy. I therefore changed my position on the spot, and now advocate the frame-securing ground rule that all supervisory presentations be made from memory and without recorded notes.

I had managed to rationalize this break in the supervisory frame for many years. In part this arose from my own inevitable residuals of frame-deviant needs and secured-frame anxieties, and in part from the fact that I had failed to listen to supervisees and their presentations with the deviant trigger in mind as the organizer of the encoded narratives that I was hearing. I am quite certain that the coincidental stories told to me by my supervisees, and aspects of the material that they selected for presentation to me, encoded their jaundiced unconscious perceptions of this frame alteration. This proved to be an excellent lesson in the maxim that if you don't listen communicatively, if you don't search for active triggers, and if you don't check out existing narratives for responses to known deviations (however well rationalized), then you don't get the encoded message and you fail to secure the frame as needed—and suffer the consequences unknowingly.

I did finally get the message and have rectified the frame with salutary results—mixed, of course, with secured-frame anxieties. Deep unconscious experience and conscious-system defensive needs are such that every psychotherapist will find himself or herself in a never-ending situation of learning new things about the treatment interaction—and themselves.

## A FINAL WORD OR TWO

You can see, then, that the strong adaptive position opens many avenues for discovery—there is a great deal there that can be used in highly constructive ways. But in the realm of the emotion-processing mind and psychotherapy, discovery is inevitably coupled with new issues, freshly discovered unsolved problems, and new sources of anxiety and concern.

As we probe more deeply into the emotion-processing mind, we are bound to come up against the limitations both of human resources in the emotional domain and of the healing powers of the psychotherapist. While I do not believe that we have, as yet, reached those limits, there is compelling evidence that real traumas can severely damage the emotion-processing mind (as they can every other organ of the body). These impairments and modifications in architecture may well be so severe at times that it is impossible to restore the mind to its full and optimal functioning.

Yet we must not give up hope. When microbes became resistant to antibiotics, we used our exceptional and creative minds to invent and discover stronger medicines. In what is termed an *arms race*, microbes then mutated and generated strains that were resistant to our best efforts, to which we are now responding with fresh efforts to gain the upper hand again. Similarly, as we see more and more clearly the damage that life's events and humans can do to the human mind, we can turn our minds—and both our conscious and unconscious intelligences—to the task of overcoming that damage as much as humanly possible. I believe that here, too, human ingenuity can win the day. It is my hope that this book has or will contribute in some small way to this victory of cure over illness.

# REFERENCES

Edelson, M. (1984). *Hypothesis and Evidence in Psychoanalysis.* Chicago, IL: University of Chicago Press.

Freud, S. (1900). *The Interpretation of Dreams. Standard Edition,* 4-5: 1-627.

Freud, S. (1923). *The Ego and the Id. Standard Edition, 19:* 1-66.

Gould, S., & Lewontin, R. (1979). The spandrels of San Marco and the panglossian paradigm. A critique of the adaptationist programme. *Proceedings of the Royalty Society of London, 250:* 281-328.

Grunbaum, A. (1984). *The Foundations of Psychoanalysis: A Philosophical Critique.* Berkeley, CA: University of California Press.

Kuhn, T. (1962). *The Structure of Scientific Revolutions.* Chicago, IL: University of Chicago Press.

Langs, R. (1981). Modes of cure in psychoanalysis and psychotherapy. *International Journal of Psycho-Analysis, 62:* 199-214.

Langs, R. (1982). *Psychotherapy: A Basic Text.* New York: Aronson.

Langs, R. (1984-85). Making interpretations and securing the frame: danger situations for psychotherapists. *International Journal of Psychoanalytic Psychotherapy, 10:* 3-23.

Langs, R. (1985). *Madness and Cure.* Lake Worth, FL: Gardner Press.
Langs, R. (1986). Clinical issues arising from a new model of the mind. *Contemporary Psychoanalysis, 22:* 418–444.
Langs, R. (1987a). A new model of the mind. *The Yearbook of Psychoanalysis and Psychotherapy, 2:* 3–33.
Langs, R. (1987b). Clarifying a new model of the mind. *Contemporary Psychoanalysis, 23:* 162–180.
Langs, R. (1988). *A Primer of Psychotherapy.* Lake Worth, FL: Gardner Press.
Langs, R. (1992a). *A Clinical Workbook for Psychotherapists.* London: Karnac Books.
Langs, R. (1992b). 1923: the advance that retreated from the architecture of the mind. *International Journal of Communicative Psychoanalysis and Psychotherapy, 7,* 3–15.
Langs, R. (1992c). *Science, Systems and Psychoanalysis.* London: Karnac Books.
Langs, R. (1993a). *Empowered Psychotherapy.* London: Karnac Books.
Langs, R. (1993b). Psychoanalysis: narrative myth or narrative science? *Contemporary Psychoanalysis, 29:* 555–594.
Langs, R. (1994). *Doing Supervision and Being Supervised.* London: Karnac Books.
Langs, R, (in press). Science and evolution: pathways to a revolution in the world of psychotherapy. *American Journal of Psychotherapy.*
Langs, R., & Badalamenti, A. (1992). The three modes of the science of psychoanalysis. *American Journal of Psychotherapy, 46:* 163–182.
Langs, R., & Badalamenti, A. (1994). Psychotherapy: the search for chaos and the discovery of determinism. *Australian and New Zealand Journal of Psychiatry, 28:* 68–81.
Slavin, M., & Kriegman, D. (1992). *The Adaptive Design of the Human Psyche.* New York: Guilford Press.
Tooby, J., & Cosmides, L. (1990). The past explains the present. *Ethology and Sociobiology, 11:* 375–424.
Tooby, J., & Cosmides, L. (1992). The psychological foundation of culture. In: J. Barkow, L. Cosmides, & J. Tooby (Eds.), *The Adapted Mind* (pp. 19–136). New York: Oxford University Press.

# INDEX

adaptation, of the emotion-processing mind, 7, 13–15, 17–27, 32–33, 62, 64, 69–71
   conscious, 7, 15, 32–33, 57–58, 60, 65–79
   deep unconscious, 7, 15, 33, 48, 58–61, 98, 103–104
   direct (immediate), 14–16, 21, 41, 55, 100–101
   -evoking stimuli: *see* triggers
   issues:
     for patients, 20–21, 26–27
     for therapist, 21–24
adaptive, viewpoint
   strong, 13, 21, 125
   weak, 21, 41, 54
anxiety: *see* death anxiety; frame, secured anxieties
architecture, of the mind [of the emotion-processing mind]: *see* mind, architecture (design, structure) of
associating
   free, 19, 25
   guided, 25, 66–68, 82–83, 91–92

Badalamenti, A., 4, 6, 32, 144
Barkow, J., 144
boundaries: *see* frame

communication, in psychotherapy, 13–14, 55
   conscious, 13–14
   unconscious, 13–14, 81, 103

# INDEX

communicative psychotherapy: *see* psychotherapy, communicative
condensation, 60, 103
Cosmides, L., 5, 6, 144
countertransference, 22

death anxiety, 57, 62, 78–79, 87, 108–109, 118, 129
decoding, trigger, 19, 45, 50–51, 58–61, 81–82 (*see also* linking process)
deep unconscious message: *see* message, encoded
defence, perceptual, 50, 75, 76, 98
derivative message: *see* message, encoded
displacement, 104–107
dream-equivalent [made-up story], 95
dreams, 10–12, 66–68, 82–83, 91

Edelson, M., 143
ego, 38, 39, 41, 80, 87, 102, 114
emotion-processing mind: *see* mind, emotion-processing
empowered psychotherapy: *see* psychotherapy, empowered
encoded message: *see* message, encoded
evolution, of the emotion-processing mind: *see* mind, emotion-processing, evolution of
experience:
 conscious, 7, 57–61, 83
 unconscious, deep, 7, 32, 49, 57–61, 83,

frame [ground rules, boundaries], 18–20, 23–25, 43, 44–50, 53–57, 59, 61, 66–69, 78, 83–88, 89–96, 99–100, 120–121, 138
 absence, from session, 62
 altered: *see* frame, deviant
 anonymity, relative, of therapist, 19, 46, 66, 92–94, 95–96, 105–106
 censorship, absence of, 19
 confidentiality, 19, 46
 and conscious system, 78, 117–119
 couch, use of, 19
 and deep unconscious system, 99–100, 101
 deviant [altered/modified], 20, 46–50, 54–57, 59, 62–64, 66–69, 86–88, 92–94, 117, 129, 139–140
 face-to-face mode, 19
 fees, 18, 46, 53, 55–57, 58
 fixed, 18–19, 46
 free associating: *see* associating, free
 frequency, of sessions, 18
 guided associating: *see* associating, guided
 holidays, legal, 46–50
 length, of sessions, 18
 meaning, related to, 83–88
 modifications of: *see* frame, deviant
 modifying, to secure, 85
 neutrality, of therapist, 19
 one-to-one situation: *see* frame, privacy
organizer of deep unconscious experience, 83–85

privacy, 18,19, 46, 53, 62–64
   rectification of (deviant), 49
   secured, 20, 85–86, 101, 117-119
      anxieties, 20, 21, 85–86, 117–119 (*see also* death anxiety)
      universal need for, 85–86
   setting, 17–19
   sound-proofing, 18
   rectification, models of from patient, 94, 96
Freud, S., 4, 35, 38, 77, 80, 113, 124, 143

Gould, S., S, 143
ground rules: *see* frame
Grunbaum, A., 143
guided associating: *see* associating, guided
guilt, unconscious, 78–79, 108–109
   in patients, 57, 62
   in therapists, 119

id, 38, 39, 41, 80, 87, 102, 114
indicators: *see* self-indicators
insight, deep, 27 (*see also* linking process)
interpretations,
   interactional: *see* linking process
   unconscious (by patient to therapist), 50
interventions, of therapist, 21–22, 130–131 (*see also* linking process)
   silence, 21–22
   unconscious meanings of, 45

Kriegman, D., 5, 6, 144
Kuhn, T., 6, 40, 143

Langs, R., 4, 6, 8, 9, 13, 18, 21, 22, 26, 32, 37, 38, 47, 97, 118, 125, 126, 138, 143–144
language, 13–14, 32, 109
Lewontin, R., 5, 143
linking process, 25–26, 48–50, 55–61, 63–64, 68, 73, 93–94
listening–formulating process, 120

maladaptations, in patients, 63
meaning, 32–33
   implied, 34–35
message:
   encoded, 13–14, 55
   manifest (direct), 13–14, 31–32
mind, emotion-processing, architecture (design, structure) of, 5, 7–9, 45, 50, 59, 60–62, 65–79, 82, 97–109, 115–119
   concept of:
      single-system, 16, 37
      two-system, 16, 50–51, 52
   dysfunctions (syndromes) of, 124–138
   evolution of, 5, 70, 76, 85, 104
   models of:
      communicative, 41–51
      structural, 38–40, 80, 113–114
      topographic, 35–37, 113, 124
   systems of: *see* system

narrative, as carrier of encoded meaning, 13–14, 47–50, 55
  origination, 25
natural selection: *see* mind, emotion-processing, evolution of

perception, unconscious (subliminal), 23, 49, 99, 105
psychotherapy, 10–12
  assessment of, 115–119
  classical forms of, 35–40
  communicative, 8, 18–19, 41–51
  dissatisfactions with, 2–3, 80, 93, 113–115
  empowered, 8, 18, 24–17, 65–71, 82–83, 88–94, 95–96
  fundamentals of, 4–8, 13–16, 35–40, 80
  techniques of (in light of the design of the mind), 119–123

resistances: *see* self-indicators

self-indicators (symptoms and resistances), 32, 83, 88, 106–107, 131–132
Slavin, M., 5, 6, 144
structural theory: *see* mind, emotion-processing, models of, structural
subliminal perception: *see* perception, unconscious (subliminal)
superego, 37, 38, 39, 41, 80, 87, 102, 114
supervision, 138–140

survival: *see* system, conscious, survival function of
system:
  conscious, 47, 52, 61–62, 65–79, 121–123
    defensiveness, 72, 75–76
    denial by, 76, 87, 136
    malfunctions of, 127
    repression by, 68–69, 77, 91, 92
    superficial unconscious, subsystem of, 77–78
    survival function of, 74–75
    vulnerability of, 75–76
  deep unconscious, 45, 47, 52, 61–62, 73, 97–109
    denial by, 95–96, 101–102, 107–108, 136
    intelligence (wisdom) of, 102, 108
  fear/guilt subsystem (of deep unconscious system), 108–109
  overload, 125–126, 128

themes:
  bridging, to therapy, 25, 48, 60, 91, 133
  power, 60, 91, 133
Tooby, J., 5, 6, 144
topographic model of the mind: *see* mind, emotion processing, models of, topographic
transference, 22
triggers, 14, 25–26, 43, 83
  conscious, 14, 33–34
  decoding method: *see* decoding process
  encoded representations of, 47

frame-related, 59 (*see also* frame)
identification of, repressed
  via direct recall, 67, 89, 90
  via themes, 67, 90–92
impression, 89
nature of, 23–24
repressed [unconscious], 14, 47, 67–68, 89–93
traumatic, 71–73, 125–130, 135–138

validation, of therapist's interventions, 22, 26
  cognitive, 94
  conscious, unreliability of, 79, 115–117
  interpersonal, 94
  unconscious [encoded], 22, 26, 64, 86, 90, 131–132
vignettes, 10–12, 33–35, 42–50, 52–61, 62–64, 65–71, 71–73, 82–83, 88–94, 95–96